Roger & Bobby

Many blessings from

my "little Talks" with

God

Peggy Rooney

uncommon conversations
with God

by
Peggy Rooney

RIVER
OAK

PUBLISHING

Uncommon Conversations with God:
Unique Expressions of Prayer and Praise
ISBN 1-58919-798-4
Copyright © 2001 by Peggy Rooney

Published by RiverOak Publishing
P.O. Box 700143
Tulsa, Oklahoma 74170-0143

uncommon conversations with God

dedication

To my family and friends.
As I witness your growth in times of
both difficulty and success, I am inspired
to draw closer to God in my own life—
to seek His wisdom, comfort, and joy.

acknowledgments

My special thanks to God for the gift of His inspiration. I also owe much gratitude to my family and friends who have encouraged and supported my dreams. Finally, I wish to thank my editors, Christina Honea and Rebecca Currington, who have been my guardian angels in bringing this book to fruition.

table of contents

*May the words of my mouth
and the meditation of my heart be
pleasing in your sight, O LORD,
my Rock and my Redeemer.*

—PSALM 19:14

introduction

At a very early age, I experienced many troubles that left me confused and scared. When my fears loomed like shadows in the night, I retreated inside myself to escape. I knew very little about God, but I began to feel drawn to Him. At first, I was ill at ease. Those first childish words I spoke into the darkness were clumsy and awkward, but a small seed of hope began to grow inside me. I realized that when I prayed to my Heavenly Father, I found great comfort.

Those lessons from my childhood would prove invaluable later. After twenty years of marriage and four children, I found myself a product of divorce, facing a world for which I was little prepared. I began talking to God often. I needed a friend I could trust. When life became unsteady, I prayed for insight. As I became more confident in my prayer life, I became more certain He was directing my choices. My hope was always renewed through my conversations with God.

These prayers were expressed in both the extraordinary and everyday experiences of my life. As a mother, grandmother, employee, and friend, I have learned there is nothing too insignificant, nor too great, that I can't tell God about. He is the best of listeners and speaks often to my heart. I am still learning, but hopefully I am a little wiser—knowing that the power of prayer changes lives. I hope these conversations touch your heart and inspire you to share all of your innermost thoughts with your Heavenly Father. Because of His love, I have the courage to say "yes" to life and to know that if I hold tightly to Him, He will guide me on my journey until the day we meet face to face and I hear Him say, "Come, sit awhile. We have much to talk about."

Peggy Rooney

the trapeze wire

Dear God . . .

My life is often one big balancing act. Some days I feel like I'm calling out to You from a trapeze wire, just shouting for You to stop the motion and let me off. This week has been a prime example of how quickly life can veer out of control. I had a horrendous deadline at work, and in the midst of my hectic preparation, the phone rang. Murray had been in an accident and was hospitalized. Of course, he was my first concern. When I arrived at the hospital, I learned that, although he was in some pain from a broken leg, his injuries were not life threatening. Thank you God for watching over him. Then, when I got home, I realized I had lost my wallet somewhere along the way. Just when I thought I couldn't handle one more thing—one more thing happened. Our dog Mitzi was nowhere to be found. I have been high on that trapeze wire this week! Thank You for being there for me in the midst of my swinging! You calmed my thoughts and brought divine order back to my life. I climbed down off the wire, took a deep breath, and put up flyers for Mitzi, called the card companies about the lost wallet, made the house ready for Murray, and completed my report. What a precious gift Your serenity is. Now, Lord, if You will take my hand to steady my balance, I'll climb the wire again.

> *I have set the LORD always before me.*
> *Because he is at my right hand,*
> *I will not be shaken.*
> *—PSALM 16:8*

color my world

Dear God . . .

What a wonderful, soul-filling day this has been! I spent the entire day hiking on this magnificent mountain. It felt great to use my muscles in a different way than usual. I inhaled fresh air and drank from clean, pure waterfalls. I was aware of the birds singing in the trees above and the tiny creatures scurrying at my feet. Being alone in nature is a refreshing experience that opens the spirit, one tired layer at a time, like a delicate rose unfolding in the sunlight. In our chaotic world, we sometimes feel reality is rush hour, fast-paced meals, and stressful meetings; but this is only a part of our reality, not the sum total. Reality may also be found in the tranquillity of nature, listening to the breeze whispering through the treetops and watching the sun go down behind the horizon while the clouds trail soft and pink. May I discover the reality that comes from sitting silently on the side of a hill as the crickets begin their nightly chorus and the moon is reflected in a stream like shimmering crystals. As I get to know You in the majesty You have created, You reveal a richer reality to me. Father, I ask You to remind me of this when I'm sitting in the boardroom in the midst of a heated discussion. Remind me then of Your blazing sunsets that color my world and the sound of Your booming voice echoing off the mountaintops in a thunderstorm.

–15–

> *Then Jesus said, "Did I not tell you that if you believed, you would see the glory of God?"*
>
> —JOHN 11:40

imperfect people

Dear God . . .

Whatever would I do without my friends?
Oh, it's not that they are any more perfect than
I am. That's part of the mystery. These people,
with feet of clay, need to grow just as I do. Yet,
somehow we are able to help each other
recognize and appreciate our worth. There are
times when we disappoint each other—times
when we make remarks that hurt each other's
feelings, but somehow we accept it as part of
the intricate puzzle of friendship. Friends don't
need to be perfect. I don't expect them to be.
My friends have weaknesses and shortcomings,
and there are many times when we disagree, but
somehow we manage to work everything out. I
guess there is a certain kind of forgiving
chemistry between friends. We view each other
with tolerance. A friend is not an easy thing to
describe, except to say that a friend is someone

who would leave a big whole in the heart if
they stopped caring. A friend is a person with
whom we can be vulnerable, confident they will
love us anyway. A friend is there for us when
others turn their backs. It's hard to make it
alone in this world. Of course You knew that,
so You created the gift of friendship . . . a
perfect mystery for imperfect people.

–17–

*Surely you have granted him eternal
blessings and made him glad
with the joy of your presence.*

—PSALM 21:6

snow angels

Dear God . . .

The word *snow* can bring about varied
reactions. In some people, it arouses feelings of
excitement and exhilaration—in others, anxiety
and panic. Children love it, adults may fear it,
and cats, well . . . they hate it. To be sure, a
forecast of snow can elicit a number of
responses. At the sighting of the first flake
tumbling from the heavens, we begin to scurry.
Little ones shout with joy, dad gets the shovel
from the garage, and most of us dash to the
nearest grocery store, just in case. But once the
food has been purchased and the survival gear
gathered, it is a beautiful sight to behold. As I
look out at the frozen earth, not one footprint
mars the pristine splendor of the frosty hills.
There is only purity as the gentle snow silently
blankets the grass, trapping the tree limbs in
glassy sleeves that tinkle in the soft breeze. The

gently falling flakes resemble snow angels, as they dance and swirl in the wind. Watching them play, with their lace skirts falling to earth like feathers, reminds me of the simplicity of Your love. There is peace in this silence—much like the peace my soul finds whenever I share my deepest feelings with You. Thank You, Father, for this picture-postcard scene. Snow symbolizes life . . . enjoy the beauty, absorb the tranquillity, but know that, come morning, the adventure begins.

–19–

I will send down showers in season;
there will be showers of blessing.
—Ezekiel 34:26

bad hair day

Dear God . . .

What a morning! First, I dropped a quart of milk on the kitchen floor, then the shower water was cold, and, of course, my hair wouldn't cooperate—no matter how much I primped and preened. And You know me, if my hair doesn't fall nicely into place, I don't feel quite right the entire day. I was already running late when my car wouldn't start, and I had to run to catch the bus to work. Of course, the running gave my already uncooperative hair a disheveled appearance. Once I boarded and took a seat, I was once more annoyed to discover that someone had opened the window next to the seat in front of me, and the wind nearly took my breath away. Now my hair truly was beyond repair. By this time, I felt pretty sorry for myself. But as things turned out, this "last straw" would lead to a glimpse of life through a renewed spirit. Just at the moment I felt myself sinking into self-pity, a young woman boarded the bus and took the seat in front of me. I watched as she struggled to close the open window. I finally reached over to help her. "Thanks," she said. "I'd hate to have this scarf blow off my head. People tend to stare. Chemo, you know." The rest of the bus trip I sat behind her feeling ashamed that I had been such a complainer. Thank You, Father, for putting me on that bus.

–21–

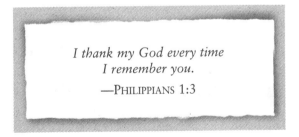

I thank my God every time
I remember you.
—Philippians 1:3

dark tunnel

Dear God . . .

Why does depression hit me when I least expect it? Everything will be fine and then, out of nowhere, my mood begins to spiral. When depression overcomes me, I feel like I'm driving a car down a mountain road and the brakes suddenly fail. Here I am again, bracing for the crash. I've been feeling so good lately, and there's really nothing in my life that's pressing right now. So why is this happening? Why am I falling down that dark tunnel where no one can reach me? It's a very lonely place. I don't want to be constructive when I'm feeling depressed, and I don't want to be talked out of the way I feel. It's absurd . . . I hate being depressed, but I don't want anyone's help. Is there some payoff in this? Am I holding on to some negative response to life that I need to release? Could it be that I am holding on to unresolved anger?

Perhaps I need to forgive someone. Perhaps I need to ask for forgiveness. I have learned one thing: With time, my mood will lift and the world will again become a place of great promise. I don't understand why these moods haunt me, but I do know that if I hold tightly to my faith and search my heart, You always come to rescue me from myself, and the experience of Your redeeming resurrection is worth the wait.

> *You will be secure, because there is hope; you will look about you and take your rest in safety.*
>
> —Job 11:18

Frankie

Dear God . . .

Thank You, Father, for sending Frankie into my life at a time when I felt so lonely and in need of love. He has been my companion now for more than thirteen years. He always understands my moods, and he never asks more of me than I am willing to give. I remember what life was like before he came around. I was withering from lack of affection and wallowing in self-pity. I was getting so set in my ways that it seemed almost too late to learn to be a congenial companion to someone else. Then Carol called and said there was someone she wanted me to meet. Oh, I must admit, at first I was not very interested and hesitated agreeing to see him. After all, I had been alone for such a long time that I wasn't sure I could reach out to someone else. But I agreed to give him a chance—I am so thankful I did. You knew just

what I needed when You sent Frankie into my
life. When he snuggles beside me at night or
wakes me in the morning for breakfast, I simply
come alive. Frankie is my constant companion—
how much joy there is when he curls up beside
me in the evenings, purring contentedly. After
all, cats are not just animals, they're friends too.
And Frankie is a fine friend indeed.

*Be of one mind, live in peace. And the
God of love and peace will be with you.*
—2 CORINTHIANS 13:11

the city garden

Dear God . . .

Moving to the city had its limitations. I
missed the expansive yard I once enjoyed. I
didn't think I would ever get used to living with
cement instead of green grass. I prayed for a
long time, even though I wasn't sure exactly
what I was praying for, but You knew. I simply
realized I had a need, and I asked You to fill it,
knowing You would understand what was best
for me. Then one day driving home, my car
completely died on a residential street. I was so
irritated. As I stood on the curb, examining the
situation, an elderly woman came out of her
house to ask if I'd like to use her phone. As it
happened, her little row house was for sale.
While waiting for the service truck, she showed
me around her home and, to my surprise, I
discovered she had a beautiful garden out her
back door—a garden right in the midst of the

city. The plot was small, but the charm and
enchantment of this cascade of sunlit blossoms
far outweighed its size. I suddenly knew I had
my garden—an answer to my prayers. Now, as I
sit here delighting in the sunlight filtering
through the dogwood tree, I realize that the
most amazing garden of all is the one that
grows deep inside me. You plant all manner of
beautiful things in my heart, and tend them
faithfully. Make my life a fragrant and
refreshing garden that brings delight to You.

–27–

*My people will live in peaceful dwelling
places . . . in undisturbed places of rest.*
—ISAIAH 32:18

keeper of secrets

Dear God . . .

I must have an honest face, because people are constantly confiding in me. Often, I feel a bit uncomfortable with the role of confidante. I used to wish that others wouldn't share their secrets with me. Carrying these secrets around and not sharing them with anyone else often seems like a heavy burden. Then, one day, I realized the full impact of this responsibility— that You have led me to this place of trust. If You hadn't, others would not confide in me. When I give people the liberty to share their hearts openly, You allow me to become part of Your divine plan for their lives. You use me to listen, to help them grow, to show Your love for them. So I have come to a place of peace with this burden of trust, and the more I allow You to use my guardianship, the more at peace I feel. I have learned to be a keeper of secrets,

because You have taught me that I can trust
You with my secrets and You will still love me.
Help me, Father, to always gather others'
confidences into the compassionate dwelling
place inside me that You have lined with love.
Help me to treat these revelations, great and
small, in the same way You treat my own. And
let me always remember that no matter what
our human secrets may be, by some miracle,
You still love us. If I learn but one lesson from
this, may I learn to mirror You in the way I love
others, no matter what they reveal.

-29-

*Listen, my sons, to a father's instruction;
pay attention and gain understanding.*
—Proverbs 4:1

Ben

Dear God . . .

When I first entered the hospice, I was so
intimidated. I'd never been around anyone who
was dying before. I was afraid I might say the
wrong thing, and I'll admit I made several
attempts before I finally passed through the
door. I don't know what I thought I'd find, but
it was nothing like I expected. The place was
bright and airy, and the staff was so upbeat. I
almost forgot why the patients were there.
When I walked into Ben's room, my insides
were quivering. Then I looked into his eyes for
the first time in months. What I saw there
surprised me. I didn't detect fear, as I thought I
might. Instead, his eyes were filled with the kind
of depth and wisdom you would expect to see
in the eyes of the elderly—those who have lived
long enough, perhaps, to be comfortable with
death. Not that Ben was looking forward to

dying from AIDS at the age of thirty-two, but he'd gone through the process of denial and anger. There was a calm about Ben that made me feel comfortable. His smile seemed even wider in a face that was emaciated. He struggled with his words. "Hi," he said. "You know how I love adventures. Well . . . this one's gonna be a winner! It took me awhile to accept it, but I'm finally at peace with it." In that instant, I felt his peace, and I knew he was right . . . this would be a new adventure. And it was okay.

–31–

> *You were once darkness, but*
> *now you are light in the Lord.*
> —EPHESIANS 5:8

fearful survivors

Dear God . . .

Many times I wonder why there is so much misery in the world. I turn on the evening news, and I'm besieged with the suffering of humankind. What's wrong with our world? You've given us everything we need for a happy life, so why do we destroy ourselves? At times, it's hard to simply get up in the morning and go confidently out into a world were the enemy lies in wait. How do we know we'll even arrive at our destination? Life does not come with guarantees, does it? Life is all about faith. I guess we are all frightened children, hovering in the dark. I suppose we are all survivors, too . . . even the perpetrators—those who have mastered boldness but not bravery. Bravery is being scared and going out the front door anyway. Bravery is knowing every minute of life counts for something and making the most of it.

Bravery is going forward in faith with no
guarantees. For only the brave will allow You
to be the strong One. I pray that You will help
me to gather enough courage to grow in faith
and survive the hard times. You are the light of
the world. You are the bright glow behind the
dark clouds, the moonlight shimmering on the
water at midnight. For even a tiny beam of
Your light, filtering through the darkness, is
enough to illuminate the path of life and guide
us—those fearful survivors—to the safety of
Your tender arms.

–33–

*Even though I walk through the valley
of the shadow of death, I will fear no evil,
for you are with me; your rod and
your staff, they comfort me.*

—PSALM 23:4

bridge of change

Dear God . . .

Why do I often find it so hard to be alone
with my thoughts? I like who I am, so why is an
extended time of quiet so difficult to maintain?
I make a thousand excuses for avoiding myself.
I am an energetic person, so maybe that's the
reason. No. I'm fooling myself again. Being
alone with my thoughts is not always easy. I'd
rather be out some place where the music is
loud and the people inattentive than sit in a
quiet room with only my thoughts. Without all
the noise and distraction, I'm vulnerable. When
I stop procrastinating and commit to my quiet
time, something wonderful happens inside me.
When the chatter stops, I can feel You
resounding in my soul. Each time I am willing
to do this, I have another glimpse of who I am
without all the words. I'm sorry I've taken so
long to reconcile myself with this gift. When I

silence my own voice, I can hear You so much better. Life continues to change. Growth as a person demands commitment. When I allow myself these times of silence, I find You waiting patiently in the corner of my heart, ready to talk to me about crossing the bridge of change.

> *Peace I leave with you;*
> *my peace I give you.*
> —JOHN 14:27

the escape

Dear God . . .

I know I shouldn't complain. My life is good. I've yet to face a problem too big to handle. I enjoy my job, it pays well, and my family is blessed with good health. Still, sometimes I wish I could experience a few exciting adventures. There are so many dreams left unfulfilled: the recognition that has eluded me, the people I've never met, the places I've never been, and the experiences I haven't had. What I'd really like to do tomorrow is take on a whole new identity, leave my responsibilities behind, and see the world. Perhaps I could fly to Alaska and mine for gold. Maybe I could simplify my life for a few months, pack the barest necessities in a backpack, and ride the rails through Europe. Excitement surges through my veins just thinking about those great adventures. But for tonight, I guess I'll

simply put away the dishes and tuck the kids
into bed. My kids—what a delight they are.
When they look at me with their bright eyes
and whisper, "I love you," I melt. Come to
think of it, my life is a new adventure every day.
I guess my dreams have come true after all. If
there is anyone who knows the joys and
challenges of being a parent, it's You. You are a
wise Father. You know that while I imagine
how exciting a new adventure would be, my true
fulfillment is right before me.

-37-

> *Each one should use whatever*
> *gift he has received to serve others,*
> *faithfully administering God's*
> *grace in its various forms.*
> —1 PETER 4:10

over the edge

Dear God . . .

I guess my daughter is right. I have gone over the edge when it comes to my grandchildren. She tells me, "Mom, when I was little, you never allowed me the leeway you allow Jessie and Gina." Of course, it's true. I was much harder on my children than I am on my grandchildren. When my children were growing up, I was strict. When I spoke, they were to listen with no argument. Of course, I gave them love, too, but I tried not to spoil them. So, my daughter is being realistic, and I need to abide by her wishes. After all, they are her children. I must keep that in mind in the future. I will stop spoiling the grandchildren so much, and I won't buy them extravagant gifts for absolutely no reason. Christmas and birthdays are the times to indulge them. I don't know what happens to a woman when she becomes a grandmother. Her whole attitude changes. It's quite a phenomenon. As I sit beside these tiny sleeping beauties, I realize that Kathy knows what's best for her children. She is the mother. I am only the grandmother, and I need to be more respectful of her wishes. I promise to do this . . .but I might need a few more years of practice.

–39–

Since you are precious and honored in my sight, and because I love you, I will. . . .
—Isaiah 43:4

Dear God . . .

The morning has been a busy one. As usual, I never found enough time to do all that needed to be done. Saturdays seem to inflate with activity, becoming a depository for everything not accomplished during the weekdays. I could already feel the underlying stress beginning to wash over me as I glanced at the clock, remembering that the bank closed at noon. I was refocusing my priorities when, from the open window, came a soft, cooing sound. At first I ignored it—*I don't have any time for frivolous things,* I thought. Then it came again. The sound drew me to the open window, curious about the gentle intrusion. There she sat looking at me, as if the window ledge held a welcome mat—this beautiful early morning dove. I spoke softly to her, "Hello, little one. How are you doing this day?" To my amazement, she did not startle and fly away, but instead cocked her tiny head and watched me inquisitively, with a kind of peaceful trust. The chores that had seemed so crucial a moment before took their proper place in real time—the time of the heart. On a hectic Saturday morning, when I needed to be reminded of what is really important in life, I searched the open window for Your gift. In Your remarkable wisdom, You allowed me to discover the trust, the beauty, and the soul-filling peace You sent to me in the special gift of Your morning dove.

–41–

This is what the LORD says,
he who appoints the sun to shine
by day, who decrees the moon
and stars to shine by night.
—JEREMIAH 31:35

Dear God . . .

What happened to my life? I just knew that when I finally married, it would last a lifetime. Of all couples, how could it have happened to us? Divorce is like a death that keeps the whole family in mourning for years. It's devastating, even when a couple tries to cushion the children by remaining friends. When did our marriage begin to rip apart? Did we neglect each other too much after the children came, or was it when the bills got out of hand? Our parents seem happy enough, and they've had hard times, too. Maybe it's the confusing world in which we live. Maybe we both just stopped trying too soon. Perhaps I should have said, "I love you," a little more. *Divorce* is such an ugly word. But I guess all I can do now is learn from it. How long must I wait, Father, before I feel a sense of esteem again? I was somebody else a few months ago. I don't know who I am right now, and maybe that's part of the problem. Transition is a time of alteration. Change so often causes confusion. Who will I be when the shock and pain begin to subside? I can only pray that You will help me to release myself from this prison of failed promises. I pray that You will help me to love again, to love from the depths of my soul rather than from my broken heart. And please, Father, give me the grace to forgive.

—43—

Let us draw near to God with a sincere heart in full assurance of faith, having our hearts sprinkled to cleanse us from a guilty conscience.

—HEBREWS 10:22

indecision

Dear God . . .

You know how I've agonized in the past when forced to make a decision. I would weigh all the facts and weigh them again. I would ask my friends what they thought I should do. Then, of course, I couldn't decide which opinion was right for me. I would even search through magazines to see if anyone had faced a similar dilemma. But there was so much advice that it made the decision-making that much harder. Then one afternoon, strolling along the water's edge, I watched as a gleaming sailboat glided across the rippling water with only a soft breeze to catch its sails and a small rudder to direct its course. That's when You filled me with Your wisdom. At that moment, I turned my indecision over to You. To my amazement, my spirit felt at peace in a way I had not known. A wonderful sense of freedom came over me. I began to trust Your guidance. I no longer agonize when faced with decisions. I simply let them rest until, in Your Fatherly wisdom, You reveal the answer. No matter how strong the winds blow to steer me off course, I place my trust in You. I let go of the wheel and allow You to guide me to that safe harbor of truth and peace where there is no more confusion.

–45–

Take the ships as an example. Although they are so large and are driven by strong winds, they are steered by a very small rudder.

—JAMES 3:4

Dear God . . .

I'm sorry I lost my temper again this
morning. Oh, no one knew about my outburst
except You and me, but after all, I am the one it
will affect all day. I need to pay attention to
what triggers my anger. The morning traffic can
usually push my buttons. I'm likely to lose my
temper in rush-hour traffic. I am annoyed when
someone rides my bumper or is in such a hurry
to pass me. But I must remember that the only
person I can manage is myself. These are simply
isolated moments in my life—only flashes in the
grand scheme of things. Perhaps we humans
resort to anger because we're afraid. It's hard to
admit our anxieties, so when life spirals out of
control, we erupt in anger to cover up the fear.
That is all the more reason to stay calm. I know
I ask this often, but I'll ask again—please help
me to relax, take a deep breath, and keep my

blood pressure down. I don't want to start my day in anger, and I know I need to pray for those who vent their anger toward me while driving in traffic. I guess that other fellow is having a bad morning too, and the best I can do is ask You to make his day more manageable. And . . . oh yes, Father, I really didn't mean what I said under my breath when that other guy cut in front of me—You know, about wishing all his hubcaps would fall off.

-47-

> *The LORD your God will be*
> *with you wherever you go.*
> —JOSHUA 1:9

wheelchair bound

Dear God . . .

    I found myself staring at the young woman in the department store today. She was very adept in her movements, though wheelchair bound. It was hard for me to watch her handle the lipsticks without offering to help—her hands were so gnarled. Her body was twisted, and she had to be strapped into the chair to remain upright. My heart went out to her, and I was so thankful for my good health. I was feeling quite sorry for her until she said to me, "I'm going to the ballet tomorrow night. Do you think this shade is right for me? I want to look my best." I guess it hadn't occurred to me that she would be interested in how she looked, much less care to attend the ballet. At that moment, I felt ashamed. She was a lovely girl with a bright smile and sparkling blue-green eyes. She must have read my mind for she said,

"Don't let this chair fool you. It doesn't keep me from enjoying life. I told my doctor not to tell me how many years I have left, for my focus is on living each day to the fullest." I had to fight back tears, not because I felt sorry for her, but because she was so inspirational. She changed my life. I will never again turn my head when I see someone with a disability. It's the spirit that makes the person, not the body. Lord, help me to live my life with that kind of courage and enthusiasm.

> *Be beautiful inside, in your hearts,*
> *with the lasting charm of a gentle and*
> *quiet spirit that is so precious to God.*
> —1 PETER 3:4 TLB

act of kindness

Dear God . . .

The employee who walked toward me seemed to be the picture of "lacking confidence." His whole demeanor shouted low self-esteem. I had purchased a large item and had no idea how to secure it to the roof of my car. As You know, I'm not very good at that sort of thing. But this gentleman knew exactly what to do. He steadied my purchase on the roof of my car and tied it securely with rope. He not only did this with precision, but he took an extra measure of time to do his job well so that I would feel safe driving home in traffic. I asked his name, then gave him a few dollars and told him how much I appreciated his good work and the time he took to help me. He smiled for the first time, and it seemed to me he stood just a little taller, as though he had gained some self-assurance. On the way home, I decided to go a step further. The next day I wrote a letter on his behalf and hand-carried it to the store. I gave it to the store manager and told him what a good employee he had in this man. The manager asked in surprise, "You wrote a letter just because he tied a purchase to your car roof?" "No," I told him, "you see, he cared about my safety—our acts of kindness have a way of coming back to us."

–51–

> *Every good and perfect gift is from above, coming down from the Father of the heavenly lights.*
> —JAMES 1:17

nowhere else to turn

Dear God . . .

The snow began falling early yesterday afternoon—the second big storm in as many days. It clung to the windows and iced the doors shut. All traffic came to a halt. Then, Debralee woke up crying, her small body on fire with fever. The electricity had failed in the night, and from the window I could see that ice encased the electrical wires. They swayed against the dark sky like chalky ghosts at play. The phone no longer worked, and all roads were impassable. I couldn't bundle her up to rush her to the hospital emergency room. It's in times like this when I realize how much I depend on You, Father. I had nowhere else to turn. As a parent, I felt helpless. I did all I could for Debralee, then I turned to You in prayer. Sometimes it takes a crisis to bring us to our knees. All through the night, I held Debralee, praying and rocking her in my arms. Then just before dawn, her fever finally broke. I was so thankful. Now, as I look out through the lacy web of ice covering the bay window, I can see a pink sunrise beginning to spiral through the purple morning clouds. How grateful I am that I can turn to You, Father, a parent Who is never helpless in a crisis.

–53–

Your light will break forth like the dawn, and your healing will quickly appear.
—ISAIAH 58:8

the gift

Dear God . . .

Visiting Grandpa in the nursing home today and seeing how much he's failed was hard on me. He looked ancient lying in that bed— withered and frail. I remember only a few years ago when he was a vibrant man with a mind and body like steel. I could hear his booming voice thundering up the front walk even before I caught sight of him, and his eyes would flash with love when he'd see me. We were great buddies. Now, those luminous blue eyes are clouded and void of light. He no longer recognizes me. That hurts so much. Alzheimer's is such a diabolical thief. It not only robbed him of his faculties, but stole his memories as well. I suppose Grandma is right, though. She says that as long as there is someone to honor them, our memories live on. Grandma has great faith. She sits beside Grandpa's bed for hours, just holding his hand and reading to him. He has always loved books. I asked her today, "How is it that you can be so calm when Grandpa has lost all his memories of you?" Her answer was a simple one. She said, "Your Grandpa hasn't lost his memories. They're carefully tucked away inside his soul. The Lord is keeping them safe until he gets to Heaven. Then, they will be the Lord's gift to him, just as the gift of sight is given to those who were blind and agile limbs to those who could not walk. Oh, the joys of Heaven!" She smiled and bent to tenderly kiss his forehead.

–55–

I will give them an undivided heart and put a new spirit in them.
—EZEKIEL 11:19

chasms of love

Dear God . . .

I am beginning to understand that grief is not simply a short process we go through after the loss of a loved one. Grieving comes in many ways, for, from birth to death, we experience many kinds of losses. Each time I lose my self-esteem, I grieve for who I thought I was. Whenever I am denied some great joy I have anticipated, I mourn in my disappointment. When someone I love hurts me with cruel words or a look of displeasure, I feel the pain of lost approval. All of us experience small, everyday deaths throughout life, and those small deaths transform us inside. We are changed people, frightened of our transformations. It is frightening to no longer know who we are. So once we learn from the challenges in life, we strive to protect our children from this same fate. Surely, we reason, they would be better off to learn from our wisdom rather than make the same mistakes. We hurt to see them immersed in their own grieving. It's a pain worse than our own. But as we grow in wisdom, we realize that we cannot protect them. They must learn to grieve for themselves—to feel their own losses and experience personal growth. Grieving carves deep chasms into the soul, but when these chasms fill with love, we begin to heal. Through Your divine resurrection, love is able to heal the bereavement we humans share in our grieving.

–57–

"Our friend Lazarus has fallen asleep; but I'm going there to wake him up."
—JOHN 11:11

Dear God . . .

Growing up, I heard so many adults talk about "those people we can't trust." Everyone was classified into either good or bad categories. I was very careful to fall into the good group. I never wanted to be like "those people." It wasn't until I was a senior in high school that my attitude began to change. Miss Stacy suggested to the class that we each become a pen pal to a prisoner incarcerated in the county jail. At first, I was leery and wrote very stilted letters. But as time went by, Jerry's letters to me told of a childhood filled with abuse and fear. He never used his past to excuse his life of crime, but he painted a picture of himself that was three-dimensional and not the flat personality I had imagined he'd be. As we corresponded, I kept thinking about when You lived on this earth, Lord. You never turned

Your back on the folks who lived a less than honorable lifestyle. Not that You condoned the things they did, but You saw the value in each person. Those letters from prison made me a better person. I no longer look at the less fortunate as though they are not credible, and when I watch the evening news and witness the suffering and destruction that human beings can cause, I pray for them instead of judging with feelings of superiority. You love us all. Each one of us has value in Your eyes. Help me, Father, to see other people through Your eyes.

–59–

"I have not come to call the righteous, but sinners to repentance."
—LUKE 5:32

promise of hope

Dear God . . .

Because of Your miraculous resurrection, we are truly changed in spirit. That first Easter sunrise marked the beginning of new life for You and for us. If all You had shown us was Your passion and death, that would have been miracle enough to realize the depth of Your love. Through Your suffering, You revealed how much value You place on Your people. But for You to go beyond death to reveal Your resurrection gives us the hope we need to handle our struggles. When we discover that hope, we come out of the darkened tomb into the rising sun of a new dawn. Even in the dark of night, You've sprinkled the sky with the cool, white lights of hope, so the darkness does not blind our vision. You are a wise Father. You know how frightened we can be, so You give us signs along the way to lift our spirits. You know we can't survive without hope. The stars fade from the heavens, and morning gives birth to Your clarity and truth. Your clarity gives us vision. Your truth gives us insight into Your will for us. It's as if the crimson flames of all our personal Good Fridays have smoldered through the darkness to resurrect in the Easter sunrise of Your radiant love. Lord, You paint such vivid pictures of Your promise of hope.

–61–

Jesus said, "Peace be with you! As the Father has sent me, I am sending you."
—JOHN 20:21

beautiful miracle

Dear God . . .

I had no idea pregnancy could be so miraculous. At first, it was hardly noticeable, even to me—until, a few weeks into the pregnancy, the morning sickness began. My stomach did flip-flops whenever I smelled food, and the scent of the gas stove sent me bolting toward the bathroom. Then, one morning, I awoke feeling like a new person. In my fifth month, I began to grow wider. That's when I bought my first maternity dress. How proud I felt wearing it! It told the world that a tiny person was growing inside my body. But the most miraculous feeling of my expectant motherhood was my baby's movement inside me. At first I felt only a flutter, as if tiny feet were tapping against my abdomen in a rhythmic dance. What a feeling! There is no way a mother can truly comprehend this miracle, but feeling this movement comes close. As my baby became heavier, the pull of gravity kept us both from moving around too much. I couldn't tie my shoes, and I thought my skin would burst. I felt waves of pain wash over me the night of her birth—soon forgotten, though, as they placed her in my arms. She was a beautiful miracle, and as I looked into her newborn face, I saw the greatest miracle of all—Your love reflected in her eyes.

-63-

> *She gave birth to her firstborn, a son.*
> *She wrapped him in cloths and*
> *placed him in a manger, because there*
> *was no room for them in the inn.*
>
> —LUKE 2:7

gift of music

Dear God . . .

The music of Chopin is romantic; Mozart, crisp and clear; and Rachmaninoff, filled with passion. But what characterizes the music of the masters is its ability to touch the souls of humankind. Music is truly Your amazing gift to us, transcending language barriers and communicating a myriad of emotions and ideas. Music that is filled with Your nature stirs the spirit, just as a walk in the woods, where chipmunks scamper through bramble bushes and wildflowers are scattered in soft colors. Music has the passion of a stroll along the seashore, calming our senses. Music is as powerful as a mountain range where eagles soar and the flaming sunrise peeks over the ridge, surprising the sleepy valley with daybreak. Music rises above the negatives of this world. When I've had a stressful day and feel drained,

I turn on the stereo, and I can hear Your voice in a symphony or a jazz tune. When I'm over-worked and under-appreciated, I can sit at the piano and play, and my burdens begin to lift. How can I thank You for the music that fills my soul? I suppose the best way I can thank You is to give this gift back to You. I pray my loving songs of worship and praise will touch Your heart—for that is music's highest purpose.

–65–

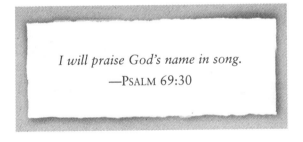

I will praise God's name in song.
—PSALM 69:30

the glove

Dear God . . .

Thank You for helping me find a way to
quiet my son's fears. I never realized that a four-
year-old could be so frightened of death. I was
startled when Johnny asked, if he were to die,
would he know he was in the cold ground? I
tried to answer his question, but my words were
too lofty for him. Finally, I grabbed a glove from
the dresser, placed it on my hand, and explained,
"This glove is like your body and my hand is
like your spirit. See, when the hand moves, so
does the glove. But when you die, your spirit
leaves your body—just like when my hand
comes out of the glove. But see, even without the
glove, my hand still moves. It's just like your
spirit, which will never die. Your body is buried
after death, but your spirit keeps living." That
seemed to satisfy my son. I could see in his face
that his fears had diminished. I felt good about

my explanation, but realized how much my children keep me grounded. Because of them, I can never be too idealistic. For later, as I lay in the darkness adjacent to the boys' room, I heard my three-year-old, Joe, ask his brother, "Could you really die?" "Yup," Johnny answered. "Well then . . . can I have your race cars?" Thank you Lord for the lessons You teach me through my trusting children.

–67–

> *My mouth will speak words of wisdom; the utterance from my heart will give understanding.*
>
> —PSALM 49:3

to touch Your cloak

Dear God . . .

As a child, I was often reprimanded for being so inquisitive. It wasn't that my elders were inattentive to my questions, it was simply that I asked too many, too often. The worst scolding I ever got as a child was when I questioned You, Lord. This was more than the adults could overlook. I was sent to my room without supper, so I could think about the offense I had committed. Well, I'm much older now, and I'm still asking questions. Somehow, though, I feel You've never been angry with me over my probing. You understand the journey I must follow. You know that I have such need to challenge life, to comprehend all things. My mind is always exploring, questioning my existence: Why was I born? What do You expect of me? Is Heaven really a place of peace? My elders would always say it's not right to

question You. But I don't mean to be
disrespectful. In the center of my soul, where
You live, I know You understand. It's not that I
doubt You. You love me, and all that You do is
for my good. But I have an enormous passion
inside that inflames my deep yearning to break
through that invisible barrier between Heaven
and earth. You are my Beloved. I will cry out to
You all my life. I will run after You until I grasp
the hem of Your cloak. And when I finally see
Your face, I will find the answers to my
questions in Your healing love.

–69–

*A woman was there who had been subject
to bleeding for twelve years, but no one
could help her. She came up behind him
and touched the edge of his cloak, and
immediately her bleeding stopped.*
—LUKE 8:43-44

the adorable hat

Dear God . . .

Today, I went shopping with my friend
Maggie to help her find a new hat. She doesn't
normally wear hats . . . and doesn't particularly
like them, but we bought one today. It's a
pretty blue denim one with a wide brim; and
right in the center, tacking the brim to the hat,
is a huge, soft pink rose. Maggie would
probably rather go without the hat, but people
stare . . . or worse, look away as though they
don't see her. So she'll wear the hat until her
hair begins to grow back. It's funny how
something like cancer can change your whole
outlook on life. Just being Maggie's friend has
taught me so much about appreciating life. She
never takes anything for granted and doesn't
worry about things that don't really matter.
Thank You, Lord, for my special friend. I ask
You to comfort and strengthen her. And help

me, Lord, to live life as she does, finding joy in the simple pleasures You give us every day. I want to sit under the maple tree and watch the children play. I want to talk to You about everything in my life and not waste a moment of precious time, to go for long walks by the lake and spend quiet evenings at home with my precious family. Thank You, Lord, for teaching me the lesson of the adorable hat.

Blessed is he whose help is the God of Jacob, whose hope is in the LORD his God.
—PSALM 146:5

gentle reminder

Dear God . . .

With two of my children in their teen years,
life resembles a war zone. I realize these years
are difficult, but I can't remember my behavior
being quite so obnoxious. My patience has
grown thin. I've prayed often for Your wisdom
and understanding. If only things were as simple
as when they were small. Those were happy
years. But children grow, and their need for
independence sometimes asserts itself ahead of
their maturity. Yesterday, Debralee cried when I
reprimanded her, and John defied me when I
told him to be home in time for dinner. After
those outbursts, I retreated to the kitchen to
start the evening meal, hoping the activity
would cool my anger. Then the phone rang. It
was Mom. She said I'd been on her mind all
evening, and she felt the need to call. I knew
right away that You had prompted that phone

call. Mom gave me a sympathetic ear as I cried and ranted on about the indifference of my teenage children. Then she gently reminded me of the time when I was fifteen and my friend Jenny spent the night. After everyone had gone to bed, we snuck out of the house through the basement window. At five o'clock the next morning, Mom got a phone call from the police. We wanted to experience our freedom, but instead ended up in police custody. I smiled. I had forgotten that episode. I asked for Your help, Lord, and in Your wisdom, understanding came through my forgotten memories.

Honey from the comb is sweet to your taste. Know also that wisdom is sweet to your soul; if you find it, there is a future hope for you, and your hope will not be cut off.
—PROVERBS 24:13-14

the small voice

Dear God . . .

I really do want to be a success. Unfortunately, things never seem to work out for me. When I went to work today, I realized the project I labored over late last night—the one that was due by 8:30 this morning—was the wrong one. Of course, getting recognition for everything I do *right* isn't so simple. I work so hard, putting in all those extra hours, and then the guy in the next office gets the promotion. I am beginning to realize how much I need You. This is the first time I've talked to You in months; in all my striving, I have forgotten to spend time with You. Lord, thank You for Your Word that reveals the truth to me. And thank You that I can hear Your still, small voice inside me, speaking words of wisdom and love. You tell me that success is more than a promotion. It's more than rising above all the others who are struggling to achieve. Success is finding favor with You when I do my very best. Success is being a loving parent and faithful spouse. A successful person is a listener who affirms others. Success comes from showing others that You are our best Friend. Help me to always listen to Your voice and to forget my own importance long enough for You to share Your Fatherly advice. For true success only comes when we hand the controls over to You, Lord.

-75-

Since we live by the Spirit, let us keep in step with the Spirit.
—GALATIANS 5:25

legacy of love

Dear God . . .

To see what miraculous creations we are, we only have to look at our family tree. I find it so exciting to see old family photos and discover how we resemble our ancestors. I have my great-grandmother's eyes and my uncle's chin. But more than the way my features resemble those old photos, it's the expression in my great-grandmother's eyes. How often have I walked past a mirror and seen that very same expression in my own eyes? It's the way my uncle held his chin, with his regal manner, that makes my family say, "Look at Peggy's chin sticking in the air so snooty, just like Uncle Harold's." The family genes are passed down through the generations like streams of flowing water. In the same way, we receive an inheritance from You. Your awesome creative power and handiwork are evident in each of us.

You created us in Your image, and the older I become, the more I see Your fingerprints on Your children—even if it is only a glimmer. My ancestors laid down a family foundation that I now build upon. What an immense responsibility! The legacy I leave will be the basis on which future generations build their lives. How important, then, that the foundation I build for my children and grandchildren is good, pure, and loving. More than mere personality traits or physical features, may I pass on Your legacy of love.

> *By the grace God has given me, I laid a foundation as an expert builder, and someone else is building on it.*
>
> —1 CORINTHIANS 3:10

new beginnings

Dear God . . .

I often view life as a continuous string of events, one blending into the next until it confuses my thinking. I often allow the debris from one situation to seep into another, wondering why I can never solve my problems with a clear head. Then, this evening, as I opened my journal to capture the events of the day, it occurred to me that life isn't the blur I thought it was. Tomorrow's journal holds a blank piece of paper with nothing written on the page, because I've yet to live it. I realized— tomorrow is just like that blank piece of paper. The page is as pure as a new beginning. After all, that's what new beginnings are—pristine and full of promise. So much planning goes into each day, and, of course, this is an essential part of living. But what would happen if I left part of my day unplanned so that You could guide my wanderings? What wonderful adventures I might have to write about in my journal! Tonight, I will write down the happenings of my day and offer them to You; and in Your wisdom, You will make sense out of my foolishness. Then tomorrow morning, when I wake to the music of nature outside my window, I'll invite You to walk with me through my brand-new day. And as evening falls on my new beginning, I will write in my nightly journal about the intimate joys we have shared.

*Stand at the crossroads and look;
ask for the ancient paths, ask where
the good way is, and walk in it, and
you will find rest for your souls.*

—JEREMIAH 6:16

best-seller

Dear God . . .

As the police brought the woman who lives next door out in handcuffs, I peered through the kitchen curtains. My first impulse was to pick up the phone and call Marie to share this interesting gossip. And she'd probably have said, "I knew that woman was up to something, coming in and out of her house all hours of the night." But as I lifted the receiver, I suddenly remembered my Bible reading from this morning and Jesus' words about being without sin before casting a stone at another. I thought about what those words meant, and I realized that they mean the same today as they did when Jesus first spoke them—that we are not to judge others unless we have done nothing for which to be judged. Well, that leaves me out. We both know I've not been that innocent. So instead of phoning Marie, I prayed for my neighbor. I'll go by her house in the morning to ask if there is anything I can do for her family. You know, I've always wondered about what Jesus wrote on the ground with His finger the day He said we are not to judge one another. With all that has been written about Him, that remains a mystery. Is that a message for our lives? Each new day is an opportunity to write another earthly chapter in the book of life. Help me to write a best-seller filled with stories of faith.

Jesus said to them, "If any one of you is without sin, let him be the first to throw a stone at her." Again he stooped down and wrote on the ground.

—JOHN 8:7-8

following Your plan

Dear God . . .

I must confess that I am feeling a lot of frustration today. Everything I had planned has fallen apart. I've had nothing but interruptions, and people aren't taking my opinions seriously. I feel out of control. Of course, I realize that when things aren't going the way I've planned, they are probably going according to someone else's plan. I guess we can't all have our way. When I allow myself to think about it, I realize that You have a plan too, and maybe when my strategy doesn't work, it's because You are directing me along another path. I suppose if I knew how many times You have saved me from destruction by changing my course, I would be amazed. I remember that morning when, just as I was leaving the house for work, I discovered one of the tires on my car was flat. You know how frustrated I was. After the tire was changed and I was on my way, I drove past a bad auto accident. It was on the route of my usual drive to work. That could have been me, except for that flat tire. Sorry, Father. I guess I complain a lot without thinking of all You do to keep me safe and on the right track. I will keep that in mind today as I struggle to replace my frustration with Your wisdom.

–83–

In his heart a man plans his course, but the LORD determines his steps.
—PROVERBS 16:9

the promise

Dear God . . .

Sometimes I wonder if growing older means having to give up all the pleasures in life. It's not fair. Through the rite of passage, at an age when I've earned the time to bask in life's joys, I find myself denied the simplest of pleasures. All I want is to be able to enjoy the foods I love. Granted, they are the foods that tend to cause me to put on weight, but they are also the foods that give what little enjoyment I have in life. And, may I remind You, they are the same foods I've eaten all these years without putting on an extra ounce. Well, I guess there is no point in debating this with You. My fussing won't change a thing. I suppose what You're telling me is that the only thing I can change is myself. I didn't want to hear that. But, I guess if I'm going to lose this excess weight, it will require some work. So why is it when the time comes that I must work harder, I'm more tired than I used to be? Okay, Lord, I'll stop complaining and start eating healthy foods and taking long walks. And I'm going to give up ice cream . . . but tonight, well . . . there is part of a half gallon still in the fridge . . . I can't just throw it out. That wouldn't be right. What a waste. But I promise, I will start my diet first thing tomorrow morning.

–85–

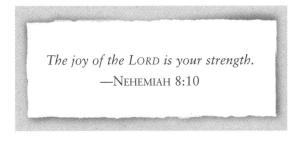

The joy of the LORD is your strength.
—NEHEMIAH 8:10

my soul to keep

Dear God . . .

Your lessons are amazing. At first they appear more like annoyances, but they're not. They're opportunities to look inside my heart and be humbled. I'll admit, when I got that second speeding ticket, I didn't think of it as an opportunity. Oh, I was grateful when the judge said to work off the points with community service, but then he added . . . in a homeless shelter. Me, work in a homeless shelter? Everyone knows the kind of people you find there. Of course, I went—reluctantly. That's when I met Shortchange and Coolhand. I never did learn their given names—but it didn't matter. During that weekend, I saw and heard things that changed me forever. Shortchange told me, "We's just like family on the streets. If anybody gives us food, we share it, just like family. Once when I was sleeping in a cold doorway, a guy tore his blanket up and gave me half. We's good friends till this day." I saw how humble everyone was who came through the soup line. Coolhand said, "Thanks, ma'am, and God bless you." Him wanting You to bless me. *I* should have told *him* that. But what got to me the most was when I left that Sunday night. The lights went out, and I heard one guy mumbling in the dark . . . then another . . . and another . . . "Now I lay me down to sleep. I pray the Lord my soul to keep." I thought . . . *just like family.*

"Everyone who exalts himself will be humbled, and he who humbles himself will be exalted."
—LUKE 18:14

ebb and flow

Dear God . . .

When I was growing up, I often felt guilty if I experienced joy in my life at the same time my friends were having problems. I tried to hide my happiness around them. After all, if they were sad, shouldn't I be sad too? As I grew older, I began to have a better understanding of what You mean by, "To every thing there is a season." Yesterday morning, as I sat at the edge of the shoreline, I watched the sun peek over the horizon to kiss the sand, leaving a tinge of pink. I was mesmerized as the sea teased the shore with the ebb and flow of liquid foam. That ebb and flow is much like how life unfolds, I thought. While one person is suffering pain, another is elated over a special event. At the same time that one person dies, a new being is gasping the first breath of life. The seasons of life continuously change. Your wisdom is never-ending, Father. Much like the give and take between sea and shore, there is ebb and flow . . . ebb and flow . . . telling me that when my friend is suffering, I can comfort her from my joy. When she is feeling the loss of esteem, I can revere her out of my sense of well-being. That must be the purpose for the seasons of life— giving to each other what we lack at the moment. How wonderful, Father, that You have blessed us with Your saving grace in the ebb and flow of life.

-89-

> *You will go out in joy and be led forth in peace; the mountains and hills will burst into song before you.*
> —ISAIAH 55:12

simplicity of soul

Dear God . . .

What a horrific storm! Why do summer
storms so often come while I'm driving home
from work? The rain is falling in sheets so thick
I can't see the road ahead, and the thunderclaps
nearly rock the car as they crash to earth. All
this chaos frightens me. I've always been afraid
of storms. I'll just pull off the road and wait for
this to pass. I feel so isolated as the wind and
rain swirl around me and lightening shoots
white webs across the sky. As I sit here talking
to You, Lord, I feel a sense of calming inside. I
can feel You giving Your peace to me. Life is
like this, isn't it? All around me the world's
storms roar, throwing me off balance, rocking
my composure. Security escapes me at those
times. People toss spears of animosity, and we
so often go to battle instead of helping each
other find a safe haven. All around me is

disarray, and it takes so much energy to sift through the debris to find my buried spirit. Simplicity of soul is the answer. No matter how much chaos is raging outside, I must find the simple fortress where You live inside me. Father, help me to always come to You to calm the fury of life's storms. The truth is that as long as I have You, nothing can really disturb my simplicity of soul.

–91–

> *The peace of God, which transcends all understanding, will guard your hearts and your minds in Christ Jesus.*
>
> —PHILIPPIANS 4:7

still unclaimed

Dear God . . .

When I view my image in a mirror, I search vainly for what You see inside me. My desire is to give You my life completely, but the face staring back at me from the mirror betrays my secret—that I am still holding back from complete surrender to You. What am I afraid of? After all, my body and soul belong to You. But still, there is something within me that rebels. Just last week, I had a wonderful opportunity to give my time to an elderly woman who needed someone to drive her to the clinic. You placed that situation squarely in front of me, and I knew it, but all I could think about was how busy I was and how there were others who could offer to take her. The next time I saw her, I felt ashamed and tried to avoid her glance. I did the same thing three years ago, when I got that desperate call from Kelly. She was so distraught. I tried to lift her spirits, but I should have driven over to her place. You were prompting me that she needed more than I could give over the phone. But I resisted, and the next morning, neighbors found her, near death, after taking an overdose of prescription drugs. I know I can't take on the problems of the whole world, but I can do my share with You in my life. There is some part of me that is still unclaimed by Your good. Help me to surrender it to You.

Now we see but a poor reflection as in a mirror; then we shall see face to face.
—1 CORINTHIANS 13:12

living water

Dear God . . .

According to Your perfect design, all of creation is sustained by water. Our bodies would die without water. The food which nourishes our bodies can only sprout and grow when the roots drink of the nurturing rain. We fish in water, bathe in it, play in it. We sail around the world over the ocean whitecaps and use water for power. When we are saddened, tears swell in our eyes as we long to understand and express our pain. Water is so vital that You protect new life in the womb with caressing fluids. But we thirst for more than the water that sustains our bodies. The water You give purifies our souls. Throughout our natural lives, we long for Your living water, the kind that does more than support our physical bodies. It's a thirst that longs to be satisfied. Without this water, our spirits would be dry and parched.

How can anything exist apart from You? In Your infinite wisdom, You set all of creation into place. In the same way that every living thing requires water to survive, You have created within our spirits a complete dependence upon You. Quench the deep thirst of my spirit with Your life-giving, life-changing, life-sustaining water . . . and allow me to bring others to Your never-ending wellspring of life.

–95–

"If you knew the gift of God and who it is that asks you for a drink, you would have asked him and he would have given you living water."

—JOHN 4:10

I can do it!

Dear God . . .

   As I sat quietly in prayer yesterday, the
room suddenly filled with palpable energy as
my little girl shattered the silence with her
laughter. In her hands she held her new shoes.
"Look!" she said with excitement, "I can tie
my own shoes!" She slipped on the shoes, and
the tiny fingers began to awkwardly maneuver
the shoelaces. She had no care that it took a
few tries to make the bow stay in place. With a
final pull, she secured the lopsided bow and
with her face beaming, exclaimed, "I told
you—I can do it! I can tie my own shoes!" Her
achievement filled me with joy, not simply
because she had learned a new skill or that she
had experienced success, but that her sense of
esteem was vividly clear and wondrous. We can
learn so much from children. They know how
wonderful life can be. There is something in

their spirits that spurs them on to claim their worth and validate belief in themselves. The ability to keep that childlike sense of wonder and to know that You marvelously make us to do great things is a precious gift from You. We must reveal it to others who have forgotten their childlike faith. With nobility of spirit and a sense of who we really are, we can shout to the world with great confidence and trust . . . "I told you—I can do it!"

–97–

> *The Spirit himself testifies with our spirit that we are God's children.*
> —ROMANS 8:16

Effie

Dear God . . .

I often watched Effie standing at the iron
cookstove, the glimmering silver strands of her
hair held in place with pearl combs. The first one
up at dawn, she would stack the coal in the only
source of heat the house enjoyed, a potbellied
stove, which, by its imperial worth, governed the
center of family activity in winter. I awoke each
morning to the familiar sound of bacon sizzling
in the fry pan and the aroma of cinnamon apples
wafting down the hall. Rolling out the biscuit
dough on the floured cutting board, Effie
occasionally brushed the flour from her fingers
onto the cotton apron she wore. She had sewn
the apron from the cloth sacks of chicken feed
delivered from the old farm market. Nothing
went unused. She worked from morning to night,
never complaining, not even when she was ill.
Effie walked with a stiff, dawdling stride. As a

child, I didn't understand that she arose most mornings to a wintry chill or to the summer dampness—both penetrating her elderly limbs. Youth only thinks of how peculiarly slow old people are. And that's as it should be. For youth will be introduced soon enough to that thief called time. Effie met life's problems with peaceful strength. I will forever remember her as a quiet teacher of humility—a memory I embrace often, especially when the world becomes too bleak. But more than anything, I remember the sweetest gift of all—the memory that lives the longest in the human soul. My grandmother, Effie, knew how to love, Lord.

You will seek me and find me when you seek me with all your heart.
—JEREMIAH 29:13

Dear God . . .

As I lie here in the dark of night, I hear a
train in the distance slipping through the night
with the low, moaning sounds of a tired soul in
search of rest. It seems to say, "My wheels are
destined to take me wherever the tracks will
lead. I must hurry." I often feel like that train in
the night, rushing head-on as if propelled by
some unseen force. Although my soul searches
for my own destination, I often allow the world
to dictate my future. "Here is the track," the
world tells me, "now all you have to do is
follow it." After all, it's not easy to go one's
own way, when following the crowd will take
you in the direction so many others are going. It
can be so confusing. The "world" says its way
is right. But You tell me to think for myself. I
read Your Scripture, and I remember with
confidence that You have given me the gift of

choice. My circumstances are behind, around, and before me, but I choose the road I travel. Though You have a plan for me, You still allow me to make my own choices, mistakes and all. What joy it is to know that at any moment I can break away from the hurried pace of the fast track of this world and rest serenely beside Your still waters.

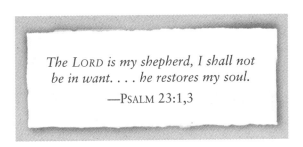

The LORD is my shepherd, I shall not be in want. . . . he restores my soul.
—PSALM 23:1,3

guardian angels

Dear God . . .

I once thought angels were wispy beings
with billowy wings reposing on puffy clouds.
Then You opened my eyes. I'll never forget that
night, driving down the dark highway,
miserably lost. I really panicked. I had no idea
where I was, and I could hardly see the winding
road. I remember praying for Your help. That's
when the brakes failed. I thought, *Is this how
You answer prayer?* The car careened out of
control, and all I could do was grip the steering
wheel and cry out to You. I've often heard that
when a person is about to die, her life flashes
before her. But all I could see flashing before me
were the enormous trees that I barely missed
hitting. I'm sure it all happened in the course of
seconds, but it seemed to move in slow,
exaggerated motion. As I reached the bottom
of the hill, there was a break in the trees, and

beyond, the black sky came rushing at me with blazing stars threatening to crash through the windshield. Then suddenly, the car, as if lifted off the road, lurched from the pavement and came to rest between the massive trees on either side of the path. The locked-in grip of the trees stopped me from going over the edge of the mountain. I sat there, too shaken to move. I felt a presence close to me and knew that You had dramatically answered my prayers. You sent Your guardian angels to rescue me.

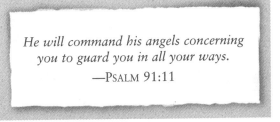

He will command his angels concerning you to guard you in all your ways.
—PSALM 91:11

Dear God . . .

The word *job* has such a mundane ring to
it. Oh, I know I need my job, and I usually
don't mind going to work. After all, it pays the
bills and puts food on the table. But retirement
looks mighty good some days—even though it
seems like a lifetime away. Why wasn't I born
to rich parents? If I were rich, I wouldn't have
to worry about a job. Of course, when I have a
great day at work and get some recognition for
a good idea or praise for a well-written report, I
feel great about my job. Then there are days
like this. Mr. Humphrey yelled at me right in
front of my coworkers. Everyone stared. I felt
like a fool. Maybe I'll call in sick tomorrow.
That'll show him. Why did I drive down this
back street? I never drive home this way.
There's always some homeless person begging
for money at the light. Yeah . . . homeless

people, people with no jobs, no food, no home. I suppose having a job is a blessing. Father, I pray for all the people without jobs who stand on street corners with makeshift signs. I ask you to send them help soon. And I pray You will show them just how very special they are to You. Thank You for my job and for reminding me of the many blessings You have given me.

–105–

Let the peace of Christ rule in your hearts . . . And be thankful.
—COLOSSIANS 3:15

Dear God . . .

The miracle You performed when You fed five thousand people with just two fish and five loaves has always fascinated me. It's almost as difficult to comprehend as eternity. What a great and blessed miracle. But, aside from the wonder of that miracle, there is a broader message in it for us. There always is. It seems You performed this miracle not only to show Your greatness and power, but as an example for us to follow. In the broad sense, whenever I help out at the food bank, I am fulfilling Your mission. When I take a home-cooked meal to the elderly lady across the street, I am doing Your will. But there is even more to Your message. When I allow my day to be interrupted by someone's need and give her my full attention, I share Your miracle. Just the other day, my neighbor caught me as I was getting into my car. I realized she was in trouble and called work to say I'd be a little late. Then I sat with her for half-an-hour and simply listened. Whenever I show kindness to others, I help You feed Your people. For when we offer each other Your spiritual food, Lord, we are ourselves a blessing, and miracles abound.

Taking the five loaves and the two fish and looking up to heaven, he gave thanks and broke the loaves. Then he gave them to the disciples. . . . They all ate and were satisfied.

—MATTHEW 14:19-20

Your Holy Spirit

Dear God . . .

I'm often confused about the Holy Spirit. Yet, I think I'm getting closer to an understanding. Sometimes I feel Your Spirit so strongly: when I'm filled with joy, when love emanates from my heart, when my day seems to flow like a quiet river. Joy, love, and peace are gifts You give us through the power of Your Spirit. I especially feel these gifts when life becomes precarious and sweeps me off balance like a wind squall. If not for Your Holy Spirit, I would be lost to life's storms. Then, there are those dry spells when my faith is weak—depressing and very lonely times. If it weren't for a revival of Your Spirit within me, I would never be lifted out of the dark pit. I remember that day last year when Sally hurt me so badly. I thought she was my friend, but she turned her back on me just when I needed her most. I had a hard time with that. I was angry, but I prayed about it. I wanted to get rid of the rage, and I knew that in order to do this, I needed to forgive. On my own, I couldn't have done it, so I prayed that You would help me to open my heart. Later, when I ran into Sally in the restaurant, I felt a softness in my heart and I knew . . . You had sent Your Holy Spirit to embrace my fragile spirit with the strength of Your forgiveness.

–109–

God also testified to it by signs, wonders and various miracles, and gifts of the Holy Spirit distributed according to his will.

—HEBREWS 2:4

nature walk

Dear God . . .

I know there's a generation gap—but age and time were fused into a mutual appreciation of life as I spent a wonderful day with my grandchildren. Only four and five in age, they are already caught up in technology—fast cars, loud music, computerized toys. When I tell them about my life as a young girl, they look at me wide-eyed and ask, "But, Grammie, what did you look at with no TV? Who did you play with? What did you do?" That's when I decided we should visit my cabin in the woods. We drove up that night and early the next morning began our adventure through the woods. At first, Rebecka and Shayne complained, "Do we have to walk far? What time will we get back?" But before long, they were completely immersed in nature. We turned over rocks and discovered a family of worms living beneath. We kept very still and listened for the unique clamor of baby birds. Rebecka, enchanted by the sunlight filtering through the trees, whispered, "Look . . . magical diamonds that sparkle!" "Look, Grammie, a baby snake!" Shayne shouted. On the way back to the cabin, we picked wildflowers in a myriad of summer colors, placing them on the kitchen table in a lovely green bottle we found along the path. That night we roasted marshmallows over a campfire, three friends who had discovered some of life's best secrets. Then, at bedtime, I read to them about the greatest discovery of all—Your love for us, both ageless and timeless.

–111–

Let the heavens rejoice, let the earth be glad; let the sea resound, and all that is in it.

—PSALM 96:11

layers of intolerance

Dear God . . .

It seems that nationality, class distinction, and cultural differences have forever divided our world. Our narrow views must be proven right no matter the cost. So, we war against each other. Brute strength replaces spiritual strength. We must seem very foolish in Your eyes, Father. After all, You created us as equals. Do we really believe we are little deities with the right to rule the world and each other? What difference does it make what we have or what the color of our skin is? All this discord will not make us worthy human beings. Our deep prejudice will not gain the control we covet. We are all Your children. We need to remember that You are a forgiving Father, so we must follow Your lead and be forgiving, too. You love us with an unqualified devotion, but we hasten through life, looking for fulfillment in possessions, in self-gratification, and in the power of our own strength. What happens when we die, shrouded in layers of intolerance? Better to inflame the candle of acceptance now than to die with cold bitterness in our hearts.

This is my prayer: that your love may abound more and more in knowledge and depth of insight.

—PHILIPPIANS 1:9

take My hand

Dear God . . .

I awoke this morning even before the slender fingers of dawn slid beneath my window shade to seize the darkness and carry it off to some secret hiding place. The sun did not beacon, and the birds were still sleeping in their soft nests. I stared at the ceiling in the dim light.

There were no illusive shadows to play with my imagination, only the awareness of my own entity. Odd, what clarity of vision there is when there is nothing to gaze upon with one's eyes. I couldn't help but think of how I hasten through life, always in pursuit of that illusive one— time—who never waits for me, even when I stamp my foot like an unruly child. Sometimes, I think I shall become very stubborn and not move until he comes to find me, but I don't . . . because I know he'll not be returning. "It isn't fair!" I shout and then catch my breath and run after him. Time does not wait for anyone. Perhaps I don't use my time wisely enough. Perhaps if I planned more efficiently, I could accomplish more in life. And what will happen when time is tired of the race? Only You know, Lord. As for me, my dearest Friend, let me rest for a moment to warm myself in the glow of Your Spirit. Then, until I feel my strength once more, take my hand and run with me.

–115–

I trust in you. O LORD; I say, "You are my God." My times are in your hands.
—PSALMS 31:14-15

blessed hands

Dear God . . .

I was struck today by the wonder of human hands—our hands perform such miracles. I thought about my hands as I went about the ordinary events of my day. I was amazed at the sanctity they rendered. I scrubbed the kitchen floor until it glistened, so my children would have an inviting place to share the cookies I had baked when they returned from school. I bathed my baby girl as she splashed water with chubby fingers, giggling as bubbles floated skyward and burst upon her tiny nose. I visited my sick aunt in the nursing home and held her trembling hand in mine. She smiled at my touch as if it connected her to the living, breathing, outside world she missed so much. When my six-year-old scraped his knee, I cleaned the abrasion and bandaged it with fingers that soothed his fears. With those same hands, I planted a lilac bush that may still bloom long after I've left the earth. I fed the cat, cooked the evening meal, and stitched a new badge on my little Cub Scout's shirtsleeve. Then, as night darkened the sky, I tucked my children in their beds as we folded our hands in prayer. But the greatest miracle that any hands have ever rendered—the greatest act of love—was when You allowed sinful hands to nail Your Son's blessed hands to the wooden Cross.

> *He touched their eyes and said,*
> *"According to your faith will it*
> *be done to you."*
> —MATTHEW 9:29

the lighthouse

Dear God . . .

I go as often as I can to the lighthouse.
Somehow the lighthouse is where I find my
passion for life. I go to be enveloped in the
powerful struggle as the sea challenges the
shore. Shivers course along my spine as I inhale
great whiffs of air. The sea rolls and crashes
against the rocks with a violent fury, but the
shore stands like an imperial soldier, firm and
unyielding. This conflict reminds me of the
clashes in my own life when hostility confronts
rigidity. One day I became aware of a small
lone figure sitting at the edge of the jagged cliff.
He seemed insignificant against the great
expanse of nature as the roaring sea engulfed all
other sounds and thrashing waves exploded
against dense rock, splashing white foam into
the air. I stayed back so as not to interrupt the
boy's solitude amidst this mighty conflict.

Perhaps he comes here for the same reasons I do. This is the place where I learn something of life's secrets. The ruby sunset was beginning to layer the dimming sky with the last radiance of day, and as the sky grew murky, I saw the boy stand slowly. Then, with the mist gleaming in his hair, the boy crouched low again and paused, as if straining to hear something within the roar of the surf. As I walked past him, I heard him say in a small, trembling voice . . . "God, is that You?"

–119–

Call to me and I will answer you and tell you great and unsearchable things you do not know.
—JEREMIAH 33:3

letting go of fear

Dear God . . .

I've spent years feeling apprehensive about life. I was afraid of not living up to expectations on my job, I feared making decisions, and You know the unreasonable fears I've harbored about my children's safety. How many times have I prayed over that? I could never relax and let go. Letting go was frightening. Then I met Irene. She was partially blind and had lost both legs as a result of diabetic complications. She had the use of only one hand, because an accident in her teens had left her right hand crippled. But Irene had an infectious laugh, the kind that comes from the heart. She was all heart, and her caring was infectious too. Since I met her, I've never been the same. She had such courage. She taught me to let go. She said that letting go simply means letting You take control. I was afraid. After all, who would protect me if I let go? I watched how dependent she was on others. She had no choice. But she did have a choice in how she handled it. Irene trusted those who cared for her. She trusted You—absolutely. That's when I began to trust You, too. I remember asking Irene how she could be so brave in spite of her dependency. What she said that night made all the difference. She said, "I figure the worst thing that can happen to me is that I might die and get the chance to actually meet the One who's been taking care of me all these years."

This is what the LORD says—he who made you, who formed you in the womb, and who will help you: Do not be afraid.

—ISAIAH 44:2

memories

Dear God . . .

If You truly live inside me, then You must
be nestled somewhere among my memories.
When I live no more, where is the proof of my
existence? There are the photo albums. But they
will take on life only when those images flood
the memory of someone who knew me. There
are the letters I have written. But what do they
mean if not read from the heart of someone
who cares? My many accomplishments are
recorded somewhere, though the masses soon
forget as other's achievements are recorded. So,
it's the memories I leave with my loved ones
that will continue to give me form and shape.
All else is merely history. When I look at my
mother's photo, I don't simply see an elderly
woman with a lovely face. I see the growing-up
years, the nurturing, the discipline, the laughter.
When I read my father's letters, they are not just

words written long ago. They touch my heart and speak to me about my importance to him and how much he loved me. When I look at my son's newspaper clipping from the day he won the game for his team, it's not just an old clipping. I remember the cheering, the pride, the love I felt as his team applauded his success. If the memories I leave with others live on inside them, then I pray those reflections will be warm and tender so that when You rest Your head upon them, You'll whisper with great contentment, "I love You, too."

As God's chosen people, holy and dearly loved, clothe yourselves with compassion, kindness, humility, gentleness, and patience.
—COLOSSIANS 3:12

the test

Dear God . . .

Your words, "Test me in this," are very powerful. When I first read them, I was prompted to gather enough courage to say, yes—yes, I will take the challenge to turn my concerns over to You. Yes, I believe You will change them into blessings. I wanted so much to give You my complete trust, but I soon discovered how precarious my faith can be at times. At first I was strong in my resolve to let You handle my concerns, for certainly my own efforts caused my footing to tread on loose sand. I placed all my cares in Your hands, but before long I weakened, perhaps because the blessings didn't come soon enough, or maybe my trust faltered—did You really hear me when I cried out? So, I resolve to begin once again to turn my sorrows over to You; but this time, Lord, I ask You to strengthen my human weaknesses so that I am not tempted to take back the problems I place in Your hands. Help me to remember that my timing is not always Your timing. My reality is limited, but if I allow You to bolster my strength with the power of Your love, my feet of clay will again tread on solid ground. I know now that when You say, "Put me to the test," You are telling me to let go of my doubts and fears and to trust You totally.

–125–

"Test me in this," says the LORD *Almighty, "and see if I will not throw open the floodgates of heaven and pour out so much blessing that you will not have room enough for it."*

—MALACHI 3:10

Dear God . . .

Life is made up of millions of stories, each one a little different from the other. When I was a child, I tried to figure out how each tiny snowflake could have its very own design, but I could never fathom this fact. It's the same with humans, only much more intricate and mysterious—no two sets of fingerprints are ever alike. *How can that be?* I would wonder. Well, Father, I am still pondering that miracle. Anyone who does not believe in You must be oblivious to this miracle of life. There are many signs of miracles in the world but none more miraculous than the scope of humankind. If we humans cannot comprehend the intricacy of how our bodies were assembled—each segment working in unison with the whole—then how can we understand our creation? Each of us, while sharing similar human reactions, is a unique individual. Each personality is somewhat different, each spirit formed singularly. So, it follows that all humans have different stories to live out. This could lead us to lives of separateness, except, in Your love and mercy, You created ways for us to connect our segregated natures. When You created us, You placed love in our hearts; and because of our need for love, we long to share the stories of our lives. We support one another, even though we may not truly understand each other's stories. If not for that support, we would wander through life as lost people. Thank You, Father, that You created ways to connect us in our separateness.

–127–

It is the spirit in a man, the breath of the Almighty, that gives him understanding.

—Job 32:8

Dear God . . .

As I sat in the park yesterday, a lady appeared, bundled in a beige coat with a mock-fur collar, though the day was sunny and the tree buds were straining to burst open like tiny jewels. The bag she clutched at her side was shabby and worn . . . much like herself. Her tired face held no notable expression, but her eyes told her story. As she moved closer, I read in her gaze all the joy, passion, and tragedy of her life. I wondered if she lived on the street. Had she once loved deeply? Was her plump form once nimble with grace? Who cared for her now as she sat on park benches, feeding the squirrels? Her world seemed reduced to a tattered bag holding only a few possessions— perhaps some paled photographs to remind her of love. Suddenly, I felt a flood of insight. The bag lady was a symbol of life peeled down to the very core. I knew that the music of youth, eternal as it first seems, will someday bolt ahead and tap a new partner on the shoulder who can dance in step. Perhaps one day I'll fold my few possessions in a crumpled bag, along with my own faded photographs . . . and remember love. Maybe I'll sit on park benches and feed the squirrels, and people will ask, "Does she live on the street?" And I'll smile to myself, because I shall be wise with age and know that You, in Your mercy, have a special place in Heaven for bag ladies.

> *"Do not be afraid, little flock,*
> *for your Father has been pleased*
> *to give you the kingdom."*
> —LUKE 12:32

a golden flame

Dear God . . .

As I sat quietly tonight, watching the
candles burn, I thought about how much I am
like those candles. Some of them favor one side
over another and use only a portion of their
potential. How often I have done this. I focus
on the latest interest and ignore other pursuits,
often getting burned out because I have lost my
balance. Some candles burn themselves out
quickly. Some have wicks that never quite catch
fire. They must be rekindled again and again.
I'm often like this with my false starts, in the
way I lose interest when life is not pursuing me
like a suitor. My prayer life is sometimes like
this, too. I feel a fervor for life and find spiritual
depth, only to lose it again. During those times,
I've prayed fervently to be renewed. Then, there
are the candles that burn straight and tall, down
through the center of their formation with great

purpose. This is me when I am positive and focused. This is me when I strive for a higher purpose, and not simply for my selfish desires. When I give myself to others, when I help another to realize a better life, I am that candle, burning straight and tall. These candles all remind me of myself . . . all portraying my struggle for growth and inner strength. When the fervor of my life dies, what will be remembered . . . a pool of wax or a golden flame that illuminated my world? Help me, Lord, to always burn with Your passion for life.

–131–

How priceless is your unfailing love! . . .
For with you is the fountain of life;
in your light we see light.

—PSALM 36:7,9

the silver bucket

Dear God . . .

I claimed my sand dune early this morning as the sunrise spilled its radiance across the playful sea. This was to be my thinking place . . . my spot for solitude . . . or so I thought. But as morning startled the soft, pink sky with the golden hues of dawn, voices suddenly drifted across the cool sand. I saw two youngsters racing to the water's edge, and I knew my solitude was short-lived. Their laughter, however, quickly turned to discord over their one possession . . . a silver bucket. It hadn't occurred to them that two buckets might have kept peace between them. Perhaps they needed the silver bucket to take them to the impasse where choices are made for good or ill. There were bitter words and tears as one of the girls handed the bucket to her friend, who disappeared down the beach, leaving her to sob. I went back to pondering my adult world as I searched the sea. In fact, I hardly noticed the small figure bouncing along the shoreline. The silver bucket had returned, brimming with gleaming, pastel shells. The two young girls stood smiling at each other with treasure to be shared. I smiled. It takes courage to tell others you need them, but life is meant to be shared. And so, dearest Lord, in the golden mornings, in the purple hues of quiet days, I shall give You my silver bucket.

–133–

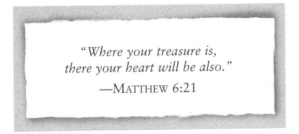

"Where your treasure is, there your heart will be also."
—MATTHEW 6:21

shadows and splendor

Dear God . . .

I stepped out into the raw air before dawn this morning, tugging at my coat collar to ward off the cold. Overhead, a neon sign was blinking . . . pulsating in rhythm with the beating of my heart. At least the neon sign gave new life to the murky puddles sprawled at the edge of the gutter . . . injecting, transforming . . . the way my soul often falters between shadows and splendor. The rain had stopped, and morning began to infuse the city like a timid child tip-toeing quietly through the mist. The night before had been a rare occasion, one where love and hate warred against each other in my heart, and I wanted to run. Early morning traffic moved drowsily, still too tired to make demands, and the sun was trying to cut a wedge through the stubborn clouds to warm the earth. I needed to feel the warmth . . . to

hear the birds singing . . . to experience signs of
hope, for last night my world changed once
again. Change is hard, Father, and often comes
so abruptly it takes my breath away. Many
times I want to hide from it, but I can't. All I
can do is hold on to You until my world stops
rocking. Right now, I seem to be standing in the
shadows of my life. But I know that if I can
hold on to You long enough, I will walk again
in the splendor of Your radiant love.

*Through the tender mercy of our
God, when the day shall dawn
upon us from on high.*
—LUKE 1:78 RSV

homesick

Dear God . . .

I visited Granddad's grave today. I can't believe he's been gone for twenty-five years. Only yesterday I was his precious little girl. As his only granddaughter, we shared a wonderful bond. Granddad was tall in stature—filled with courage and strength. He was my hero. I remember when I was just four years old, Mama sent me to spend a few weeks with her cousin in Big Bear. Cousin Penny was a good person and tried her best to make me comfortable and contented. I wanted to please Mama and I didn't want Cousin Penny to think I didn't like her, but I was homesick. I didn't know at the time what I was feeling. I simply knew that the longer I was there, the more ill I felt. I was so sick, I was scared. When I couldn't get out of bed, Cousin Penny called for the doctor to come. Later, as he was leaving, I heard him tell her, "The only thing wrong with that child is homesickness." I guess she called home, for the next thing I knew, I heard a car door slam and Granddad's booming voice, asking "Where's my little girl?" Where only a moment before I had been too weak to move, in that instant, I rolled out of bed, ran down the stairs, and leaped into Granddad's arms. He was my first image of You, Father. If Granddad could give me such love, how much greater is Your love for me? I will never be homesick again—as long as You are with me.

–137–

> *"Now is your time of grief, but I will see you again and you will rejoice."*
> —JOHN 16:22

heroes

Dear God . . .

I stepped out into the crisp, winter night and pulled up my knit scarf to keep the air from pinching my cheeks. I feel winter's cold more each year, Father. I walked at a casual pace, listening for the usual sounds. There were none. The night was silent, as if holding its breath. The glow from the street lamp filtered through the barren trees, icy branches glistening. Then, a gentle breeze began to ripple the crystal limbs with sounds as delicate as butterfly wings. Moisture flicked across my cheek. The night sky began to feather with snowflakes puffing to earth like tiny parachutes. They frolicked and played, but as they touched the earth, they disappeared. I thought, how sad to have come all this way only to vanish. But then, I noticed that where the snowflakes had melted, miniature streams of water rolled off the concrete and trickled slowly toward the faded winter grass. I was wrong. The snowflakes hadn't vanished. They gave their substance back to life. Because of them, the earth will renew itself in the spring. It's heroic in a way. I sometimes feel we are all like the brave snowflakes. Each one unique—we come to earth to blend into the melting pot with others. We frolic and play, but in the end, we must give our substance back to life. And even so, we must live and dare to love and give ourselves— to melt into the lives of others. Such heroes.

–139–

You shall be like a watered garden, like a spring of water, whose waters fail not.
—ISAIAH 58:11 RSV

the manger

Dear God . . .

The trappings of the holiday season are everywhere. I love the signs of Christmas: familiar music, twinkling lights, holiday cookies, exchanging Christmas cards. This is a time of simple pleasures. People smile more freely. Family members reconnect with one another. Excited children give hints to their parents about the gifts they hope to receive. Everyone seems more lighthearted. And I love shopping for the Christmas tree, picking just the right one, the scent of pine filling the house. But nothing compares with going to church and kneeling before the manger. This is the balance we need with all the other outward signs of Christmas. As a child, I remember walking down the aisle of the church, holding Mama's hand. She would lead me to the manger, and we'd kneel down to pray. I'll never forget that tiny baby Jesus or the radiant expression on Mama's face as she gazed joyfully at the nativity scene, light from the candles flickering in her eyes. I knew, even then, that the heart of Christmas was in that vision. Other outward signs give us great happiness, but if the trimmings are all we have, the exuberance fades as the ornaments are packed away and the tree is hauled out to the street curb. When we seek You at Christmas, and all through the year, we shall never forget that You sent Your Son into the world to save us from our sins by sacrificing His very life.

–141–

In him was life, and that life was the light of men. The light shines in the darkness, but the darkness has not understood it.

—JOHN 1:4-5

Dear God . . .

All summer I've felt discouraged. Nothing seems to be working for me. I've tried hard to hold on to hope, but there are those times when even hope eludes me. Then yesterday, as I went for a walk to clear my head, I made a miraculous discovery. I took my time going home. As You know, I'm trying harder these days to relax. I decided to go through the back alley to my yard. The city had poured fresh asphalt a few weeks ago, and I wanted to see how it looked against my white picket fence. As I crossed the alley, I nearly stumbled over a tiny, yet amazing miracle. There was a small crack in the center of the asphalt, and struggling through that crack was the fragile stem of a flower wearing a hat of sunny yellow petals. I thought, what do I possibly have to worry about? Here is a delicate entity, covered by asphalt and obscured by darkness, where no life should be able to flourish, yet this courageous flower lived. It struggled to find the crack in the road and stretched itself upward until it reached the sunlight. Surely, if this little yellow flower can reach for hope, I can do the same. Lord, I will continue to reach out for You, even if it seems there is no light. That brave flower is a symbol of creation, and You, Father, are my Light of hope.

In paths that they have not known I will guide them. I will turn the darkness before them into light, the rough places into level ground.

—ISAIAH 42:16 RSV

our Father

Dear God . . .

Our Father, Who is in heaven. To think that we can call You, "our Father." That means You claim us as Your children. We are a reflection of You, created in Your image. Hallowed be Your name. How many times do we use Your name in derogatory ways? How foolish. Your name is part of our very redemption. Your kingdom come, Your will be done on earth as it is in Heaven. No matter how much personal power we seek, this is Your world; and when we have the courage to submit to Your will, joy will follow. Give us this day our daily bread. Each day we receive our needs, along with Your love. Both sustain us in body and soul, but we must share those gifts with others. Forgive us our trespasses as we forgive those who trespass against us. When we are truly sorry, You forgive us for all things, Father. But we must go beyond

ourselves and extend forgiveness toward fellow
humans, even people we dislike. Lead us not
into temptation, but deliver us from evil. There
are so many temptations in this world. True
strength comes through Your Holy Spirit alone.
Grace us, as You did Your disciples, with the
strength to walk away from evil. For Yours is
the kingdom, the power, and the glory. Once
we can live on earth as it is in Heaven, we
discover that true power and glory is found
only in You. Amen.

> *One of his disciples said to him, "Lord,*
> *teach us to pray. . . ." He said to them,*
> *"When you pray, say: 'Father,*
> *hallowed be Your name.'"*
>
> —LUKE 11:1-2

Dear God . . .

I thought I would be devastated when I attended Uncle Matt's wake. I knew Mom was hurting, losing her only brother, so I braced myself for a painful evening. Of course, I felt sad, especially seeing Uncle Matt lying in the casket. I was uncomfortable. I couldn't wait to leave. Then the atmosphere changed. Friends began telling stories of the funny things Uncle Matt had said and done. I had never heard those stories. I knew my uncle had a good sense of humor, but I never imagined that a person's humor could be left as a legacy. Before I knew it, I was laughing right along with them and so was Mom. The laughter fused with the sorrow to create a bittersweet atmosphere in the room. After all, life is like that, isn't it? While we mourned the loss of Uncle Matt, the simple remembrances of his special qualities and funny stories about him helped soothe the pain and blessed each one of us. His stories helped us to let go because, through them, we knew that he would always be with us. That realization will stay with me the rest of my life. For humans to be capable of such a grand sense of humor in the midst of life's perils could have come from only one source—Your gift to us, Lord.

> *Pleasant words are like*
> *a honeycomb, sweetness to*
> *the soul and health to the body.*
> —Proverbs 16:24 rsv

who we are

Dear God . . .

    As I read Scripture this morning, I kept
going back to 1 Peter 3:8. I thought about my
family as I read this verse. The passage presents
an ideal for family life, but it isn't always that
easy. Oh, there are times when we seem to
reach that pinnacle: vacations at the ocean,
birthday celebrations, weddings, the birth of
children. But a family can't spend all of its time
commemorating special occasions. Between
those extraordinary times, there is ordinary
living, when the grown-ups don't always feel
like interacting, the teens are moody, the little
kids disruptive—and when Grandma locks
herself out of the house again. Ordinary living
can be a big aggravation. I used to wish we
could have a party every day, but as I got older,
I realized that's not realistic. Family members
aren't always perfect in spirit, but family is not

about perfection. Family is about being a good listener when someone needs to talk. It's about encouragement when a family member is down. It's about straight talk when needed. It's about disagreements, times of unity, and loving one another though we differ in our thinking. The family is where we learn to be who we are without pretense. They won't allow pretense, because they've lived through our temperaments and experienced all our moods. How much easier to face the world together, when we know that the head of our family is our Heavenly Father.

> *Finally, all of you, have unity of spirit, sympathy, love of the brethren, a tender heart and a humble mind.*
>
> —1 PETER 3:8 RSV

reflecting God's radiance

Dear God . . .

How often, Lord, as we read Your Word or hear it spoken in church, do we come away feeling that we are reflecting Your radiance? Not often enough. We forget, sometimes, that Your commandments are not just rules and regulations that we must follow, but they provide the models from which we are to mold our lives. You lay them out before us, but we often rewrite them to serve ourselves rather than You. I often forget. This is why it's important to read Scripture, to spend time every day in prayer and communion with You. Being human, we need to fortify ourselves daily—to fill up the empty spaces that the stresses and disturbances of this world create in our souls. I think of the radiant faces of my children when they awaken on Christmas morning to the shimmering tree and the gifts wrapped in shiny paper. Those faces don't just reflect the anticipation of what they will receive. They also reflect the gifts they have already received from You—the wonder, the amazement, the awe— that we grown-ups lose touch with all too often. Their faces show a radiance that shines from within. It seems their souls see You more clearly than ours, which have lived so much longer in this world. Help us, Father, to be more like children, reflecting the brilliance that You place within in our souls.

> *When Moses came down from*
> *Mount Sinai with the two tablets*
> *of the Testimony in his hands, he was*
> *not aware that his face was radiant*
> *because he had spoken with the LORD.*
>
> —EXODUS 34:29

summer storm

Dear God . . .

I had flashes of insight while waiting out the storm under that bridge today. Summer storms have always fascinated me—the lightening, the thunder, the raging winds, the flooding rains. But this was the first time I had been caught in a storm where I had little shelter to protect me. I felt scared and vulnerable. My life could have been snuffed out in an instant, and I knew it. Up to that point, I thought I was pretty invincible. I'll never forget that pivotal moment when You taught me about Your Holy Spirit. Just a few minutes before the storm, the sky had been clear and sunny. Then, from nowhere, the clouds rolled in and engulfed the valley. I crouched under the bridge, holding my ears. The sound was like a freight train barreling down the road. Lightening spears harpooned the ground, and blasts of thunder careened off the hills, reeling toward me like screams from a spooky movie. I questioned—*Is this how it is to be born of the Spirit?* Does Your Spirit come as swiftly as a summer storm? I can't see Your Spirit, but the Bible promises that if I invite You to live within me, my own spirit will be transformed and life will take on the peace that follows a raging summer storm. I don't know where the wind comes from or where it goes. But this day, Your Spirit was riding the winds and caught me unaware like a summer storm.

–153–

"The wind blows where it wills, and you hear the sound of it, but you do not know whence it comes or whither it goes; so it is with every one who is born of the Spirit."

—JOHN 3:8 RSV

the angel box

Dear God . . .

Memories flooded my heart while cleaning
the attic this morning. I found the metal box I
had given Kathy when she was four years old,
after her cardboard box had become tattered. I
had told her, "This is a special box. If you keep
your treasures here, they will be protected by the
angels." So she called it her "Angel Box." I was
so busy with my job that I never asked about the
treasures in her special box. I figured they were
just kid's stuff. Once she wanted to show me her
collection, but I was hurrying off to a meeting.
She never tried to share them with me again.
Now my daughter lives a busy life hundreds of
miles away, and I see her all too seldom. I
opened the lid of the box and found a rabbit's
foot and a silver comb. She had saved one of my
old rings. There was a glass slipper from her
doll, a gold plastic bracelet, and a flower pressed

between cardboard. In a faded envelope was a wrinkled letter from her father. If only I had opened that box years ago when we could have shared her treasures. But maybe it's not too late. I'll call Kathy this evening. We can talk about her treasures, and I'll tell her about the other discovery I made—that within each of us there is a special "Angel Box" with treasured memories. Thank You for these memories.

–155–

"The kingdom of heaven is like treasure hidden in a field. When a man found it, he hid it again, and then in his joy went and sold all he had and bought that field."
—MATTHEW 13:44

on eagles' wings

Dear God . . .

I am trying to understand why I pray so often, only to wait years for an answer. I see people becoming impatient when what they've asked for doesn't materialize in months. They don't know what it's like to wait for years for answered prayer. I know I sound like a child

and not an adult, but patience is still hard for me. I am trying to look at it from Your point of view, Lord, but my foresight is so limited. Oh, You do save me when I'm in desperate need, and I'm sure You have often rescued me from the dangers I unknowingly bring on myself with my foolish ways. My friends tell me I remind them of the damsel in distress in *Perils of Pauline*. I'm tied securely to the railroad tracks and just as the train comes speeding around the bend, I am saved in the nick of time! I'll have to admit, in retrospect, it creates

some exciting adventures, but I think I am
ready to mount up with eagles' wings. Even a
sparrow's wings would do. I'll start small.
Lord, I don't mean to complain. I am grateful
for Your help, and I know You have Your
reasons for the long wait in answering my
prayers. It's just that, if You're going to answer
them anyway, couldn't it be a little sooner? As I
said, my vision is limited and You know where
I need to grow. I can accept that . . . but can
we talk about some wings?

*They who wait for the LORD shall
renew their strength, they shall
mount up with wings like eagles,
they shall run and not be weary.*

—ISAIAH 40:31 RSV

Dear Lord . . .

Tears always spring to my eyes when I read about Your Last Supper. How courageous. You knew Your destiny, but You chose to do what was needed to save us from our own destruction. That was not only brave and selfless, but the ultimate gift of love. You must have hurt so much to know Your friends would deny and betray You. I can't help relating the Last Supper to my life here on earth. Knowing what You went through for us makes it easier to cope with life's problems. We come into this world with curiosity, trust, and joy in our hearts; and as we grow, we have big dreams for a life of success and happiness. But along the way, many obstacles overwhelm us to lessen our successes and fade our dreams. In the midst of it all, some of the people we consider friends turn their backs on us in betrayal. The one certainty that keeps me on track—the one reality that I ponder almost every evening at dinner—is that this meal could be my last supper. Do I want to look into Your eyes and confess that I didn't work hard enough for my dreams, that I didn't love with an open heart or forgive as You forgive? I'm thankful that You gave us this model of love to follow. You provide the direction we need to carry our crosses.

When the hour came, Jesus and his apostles reclined at the table. And he said to them, "I have eagerly desired to eat this Passover with you before I suffer."

—LUKE 22:14-15

future plans

Dear God . . .

Searching through the antique store proved interesting. I love historical pieces, mostly because of their fascinating stories or, at least, the perceived stories behind them. I especially love old photographs, even if I don't know the names of the people in the photos or how they've lived. All of them have a story to tell. You can see it in their faces. These were real people with lives much like my own, only set in a different time and place. It makes me wonder if, after I die, people will look at old photos of me and wonder what my life was like. Thinking about this puts life in a different perspective—it takes my eyes off myself so that I see life in a whole new realm of what we call time. How small I feel, thinking of myself in that vast scope. But it doesn't make me feel insignificant because I am important to You. I realize that my life is not Your only focus. I am part of a broad family of people—those from the past, the present, and the future. We are all important to You. That makes my future seem much more manageable, because if I follow Your plan for my life, then the outcome will be significant— my purpose will be fulfilled. Thank You for including me in Your amazing eternal plan.

> *"I know the plans I have for you,"* *declares the* LORD, *"plans to prosper* *you and not to harm you, plans to* *give you hope and a future."*
> —JEREMIAH 29:11

the innocent

Dear God . . .

Our world is not always protective of the
innocent in life—the children, the aged, those
with handicaps, the emotionally ill. Instead of
sheltering them, we wish they would go away,
so we could live without the added burdens.
We love the "beautiful" people, the rich and
famous, the powerful and influential. We
express hero worship over our sports figures,
even if their lifestyles are not all that heroic. We
give acclaim to powerful officials we consider
authority symbols, even though we know some
have personal lives that are decadent. Many
parents have given up the kind of parenting that
will direct their children toward an honorable
adulthood, defaulting their responsibility to
schools and teachers. What are the answers?
Do we stand by helplessly and watch our world
wound the innocent? I'm just one person, but I

can get involved in my community's activities. I can become a mentor. I can help the less-fortunate. But the most powerful weapon I have is prayer. I must pray for the innocent. But I must go a step further and pray for the perpetrators as well, regardless of how much I resent them. For when we pray together for people in our distressed world, we employ the most powerful force for change and unity. And such is the kingdom of God.

–163–

"Let the children come to me, and do not hinder them; for to such belongs the kingdom of God."

LUKE 18:16 RSV

the duffel bag

Dear God . . .

You made the heavens and the earth, and
when You completed Your work, You said that
it was good. Too bad we couldn't have been
present at that moment. Maybe we would have
been inspired to care more about our world.
Instead, we take it for granted. We are spoiled
children who have been given every advantage,
only to want more. We use Your gifts without
thinking of what we might be doing to the
generations that follow. This is their world, too,
even if they have not yet arrived to claim it. We
cut down trees without planting new ones. We
contaminate the waters with poisons. We
endanger the wildlife that is so precious to You
and so vital to the balance of our earthly home.
Last week I saw an elderly woman walking
around town carrying a duffel bag. I watched
her go about picking up cans and bottles,

stuffing them into the bag. When she passed, I couldn't help asking why she was out in the heat of the day, gathering debris from the streets. She said, "Somebody's got to do it. Somebody's got to get rid of the trash, to put it in a recycle bin, or it will pollute our town." I'm very careful now to dispose of recyclable materials in their proper place. And I find myself picking up debris whenever I come across it. That old lady's caring made me more conscious of my small part in protecting the miracle of Your creation.

> *God said, "Let the water under the sky be gathered to one place, and let dry ground appear." And it was so. . . . And God saw that it was good.*
> —GENESIS 1:9-10

Dear God . . .

I never thought of Jerry as anything but ordinary. He's the kind of person who blends in—who doesn't stand out in a crowd. He's always been quiet and unassuming—certainly not the heroic type. So when he saved that little boy from the fire, I was stunned. Who would have thought of Jerry as a hero? After all the chaos quieted down, I talked with him about it. I asked how he came to the decision to rush into that burning house, flames shooting out of doors and windows. He thought for a minute and said, *"Possessed* is a good word to describe it. On my own, I never would have had what it took to save that little boy. I stood there in front of the burning house, looking up at the windows. The fire trucks hadn't arrived, and there were very few people on the scene. I saw the boy at the window. He was screaming for help, terror in his voice. God just grabbed hold of me inside. Suddenly, I was somebody I had never been. I knew I had to save that boy from the fire. God overruled my natural fears, if only for an instant." I was amazed as he spoke. I guess this proves again that when You are in charge, we can do anything. I suppose that's how You do a lot of Your work. You take ordinary people and awaken the hero in them, so they're able to do extraordinary things.

Be renewed in the spirit of your minds, and put on the new nature, created after the likeness of God.
—EPHESIANS 4:23-24 RSV

Dear God . . .

I must be the most blessed person in the world to have been born to my mother. When You create mothers, You give them special qualities, so they can help You to nurture new life. My mom has those qualities. She has always been a model for Your Beatitudes; her kindness, her strength, and her devotion could only have come from Your love. She has been the kind of mom that I could talk to about anything, and her wise insight guided me from infancy to adulthood. Now she's a great-grandmother—almost ninety years of age. It hurts me to see her struggle with aging. It bothers me that she is in pain and that her memory is fading. She was so vital as I was growing up. Those fingers, once adept, taught me to play the piano; now they are swollen and gnarled from arthritis. Her shoulders, once proud, are bent forward as her spine has become weaker and weaker. Her vision is so poor that it's hard for her to read. But she never complains. When I ask how she's doing, she says, "The Lord takes care of me, and that's good enough for me." Lord, I know one day she will go to live with You, and I've accepted that. But may I ask one thing of You? When the time comes, please send Your most gentle messenger to take my precious mother home.

Set an example for the believers in speech, in life, in love, in faith and in purity.

—1 TIMOTHY 4:12

journey to the mountain

Dear God . . .

Looking back over my life, I can see the personal growth I've experienced, both emotionally and spiritually. I imagine it's the same feeling one has after conquering a towering mountain peak. Looking back over the valley, I can see where I've come from and the long journey I have taken to reach the summit. I've had many mountains to scale in my life. Some have been only small inclines; but how many times I have lost my footing on those slopes, sliding, having to fight my way back a second time. I would finally make it, only to discover a greater mountain yet to be scaled. It has often taken me years to conquer the great mountains that have been put in my path. I have wanted so much to give up, to retreat back to the familiar valley; but something inside has pushed me on until finally, exhausted, I have reached the top. I

have been winded but filled with renewed
strength for my accomplishment. During each
one of these climbs, I have uncovered another
layer of self, another depth of soul that I had not
identified. All along, You have waited patiently
for me to discover my way. You have gently
prodded and held my hand, pulling me along
when I have been weak or too tired to go higher.
Now, after much struggle and many failures, I
realize that each climb has added to my inner
growth. I know now that You have been guiding
me on a journey of the soul, and every mountain
I have scaled has brought me closer to what You
created me to be.

–171–

> *There before me was the glory of*
> *the God of Israel, as in the vision*
> *I had seen in the plain.*
>
> —EZEKIEL 8:4

Your unruly children

Dear God . . .

You have given each of us a free will, and we are to use our consciences to guide our decisions. You have given us the freedom to make those decisions as we see fit. But many times, conscience does not adequately prepare us to be decision-makers. We may think our conscience is leading us, but often it's simply the trends of society. The world has told us we are free people and, because this is true, we have the right to do as we please, to make our own rules and combat anything that cramps our personal freedom. Society tells us that there is no such thing as sin—past generations must have been deranged to believe so. We should not be held accountable for our actions—something or someone caused us to do it. It's as if a kind of intoxication has impaired our reasoning. We need to respect

our free will as You respect it; You honor us
by setting us free. But You have expectations
of us. You encourage us to come to You before
making decisions. You ask that we honor Your
commandments by living in holiness. You
implore us to consider others and how our
lives influence theirs. Yes, we have freedom,
but You ask that we come to You to learn how
to use the free will You have so generously
bestowed on Your unruly children.

*The law of the Spirit of life in
Christ Jesus has set me free
from the law of sin and death.*

ROMANS 8:2 RSV

our cunning foe

Dear God . . .

Down through the ages, the world has suffered the torments of an evil that lurks in the shadows and seeks to ambush us when we least expect it. It has happened to me, so I know how it feels. Evil is such a frightening foe because it so often comes masquerading as a friend.

Sometimes we befriend evil when it promises to boost our self-esteem or ease our emotional pain. At other times, it fills the void of our desperate search for love. We buddy-up with evil when we seek revenge. We cultivate its friendship as we follow false role models or feel that self-gratification is more rewarding than helping others. What frightens me is that even when I refuse to give in to evil in my own walk, it can still plague me through the lives of those I love; and I often feel helpless to stop it. When people deny Your existence and importance and give in to the temptation to embrace evil, the inevitable result is destruction—greed, abuse, hate crimes, unspeakable suffering. We can't predict what might happen tomorrow. Even though we pray for protection, tomorrow is still a mystery. So we must learn that after coming to You in prayer, we need to let go and allow You to direct our paths. Life can be unsteady, but our one security comes from trusting You totally. Whatever life brings, Your arms are always open to carry us to safety.

He tends his flock like a shepherd:
He gathers the lambs in his arms
and carries them close to his heart.
—Isaiah 40:11

the habit of prayer

Dear God . . .

The older I become, the more aware I am of my habits. Of course, there are good habits and there are bad habits—those bad habits that drive everyone crazy. When I was young, I would bite my nails. Mom tried to break me of that habit. She made me wear gloves, and sometimes she dipped my fingers in cayenne pepper. When those things didn't work, she would get so exasperated that she'd send me to bed without supper. I didn't mind. I would simply chew on my fingers. As I got older, I traded that habit for talking on the phone all evening. Mom really got aggravated with me for that too. I guess all humans form habits of one kind or another, but when those habits become hurtful to ourselves and others, it's time to take stock. When we allow our tempers to flare or consistently get agitated while driving in traffic, those habits can hurt. When we abuse alcohol or drugs, those habits can destroy our world. People say they can't stop, that their habits are too overwhelming. But we can trade one for another. By cultivating the habit of praying each time we are tempted, the habit of prayer will soon overcome the harmful patterns. It's hard to break a habit, but it's worse when we allow a habit to break us. The best way to purge those addictions is to replace them with the habit of receiving Your redeeming grace.

–177–

I love you, O LORD, my strength. The LORD is my rock, my fortress and my deliverer.

—PSALM 18:1-2

the tapestry

Dear God . . .

When I was growing up, I would say to
Grandma, "A penny for your thoughts." She
would say, "They're worth a whole lot more
than a penny." Then she would tell me a story
from the past. Even if I'd already heard the
story before, it was still exciting to hear stories
about family members I knew only through
photos. The past seemed so real to me because
it was real to Grandma—perhaps more real
than the present. She had lost many of her loved
ones, and though she dearly loved her family
and friends still with her, there was often a
wistful expression in her eyes—as though her
memories allowed her to understand and long
for eternity. Grandma died peacefully, finally
united with those who had gone before her.
Now I share the same familiar family stories
with my own children. I tell them how

important it is to remember those we have loved and to share their stories. What wondrous threads each of their lives are, interwoven like fine threads into a beautiful family tapestry. That must be how You see us, Lord. As Your children, we are intertwined and connected as an eternal family—Your family. Each one of us is unique, special, and important to You. You are weaving our lives together into the most beautiful, everlasting tapestry ever created.

–179–

You are a chosen people, a royal priesthood, a holy nation, a people belonging to God, that you may declare the praises of him who called you out of darkness into his wonderful light.

—1 PETER 2:9

going home

Dear God . . .

Since I have to watch my cholesterol, I seldom go into a fast food establishment. But I'm happy I gave in to that urge today. If I hadn't, I never would have witnessed that older couple's love for each other. They had to be close to ninety, two frail figures sitting across from each other in a booth, sharing lunch. My first thought was to pity them. They were at the end of their lives. What could they possibly have left that warranted quality of life? But the longer I sat there, the more I realized how wrong I was. I could tell that every minute they spent together was quality time. The wife seemed more fragile than her husband, and I was a bit awed by his solicitude toward her. When she had trouble unwrapping her sandwich, he peeled back the paper. Then he reached across the table and gently patted her hand in support. As she dribbled her milkshake down her chin, he tenderly took his napkin and wiped away the spill. I guess I thought of older couples as cantankerous. I had no idea of the deep love and concern older people can have for one another. Watching them I thought, *The excitement of young love is grand, but how many of us experience mature love, the kind of love they have for each other—love that truly affirms the beloved?*

–181–

> *For this reason a man will leave his father and mother and be united to his wife, and they will become one flesh.*
> —GENESIS 2:24

mirror image

Dear God . . .

When I look in the mirror, I can see You looking back at me. As You know, it wasn't always that way. In the past, I would look at myself in a mirror and see someone staring back at me that I hardly knew, much less liked. That mirror image was also reflected in those with whom I came into contact. I would either see what I liked about myself in someone and be attracted to that person, or, more likely, I'd see in others the characteristics I deplored in myself and immediately disliked them. Conversely, I would admire people because they displayed the attributes I wished I possessed, and I would try to imitate them. It was all about me. But I can't be too hard on myself. It was part of learning and maturing. Finally, when I had gone as far as I could on my own, You intervened. I remember it vividly. I was combing my hair and looking at myself from all sides when suddenly, I looked past the superficial exterior and saw Your light shining within me. I was startled. I had never seen myself like that before. After that experience, I began to notice that same light in others. That's when I became conscious of what others see in me. It's so much more important that they see You mirrored in me—more of You and less of me.

–183–

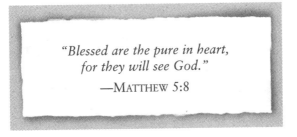

"Blessed are the pure in heart, for they will see God."
—MATTHEW 5:8

the laundry connection

Dear God . . .

I know it's a blessing that Joe is in college. I
haven't lost him. We're not estranged. He hasn't
left the country. Still, why do I feel so lost? I've
only to pick up the phone to hear his voice, and
when he needs something, I'll be the first one he
contacts. I guess it's the "empty nest" feeling
many mothers experience when their last child
leaves home. I put up a great front at the
university that first day . . . I wanted to be a
cool mom. Yet my mind registered every detail
of his room and his roommate—it's so hard to
let go. I suddenly felt useless. I went home and
sat in his room for an hour, drinking in his
uniqueness from the familiar surroundings. I
could see the little boy who waited each night
for me to tuck him in bed. I could hear his
prayers . . . how he blessed each of us. I
remembered the giggles when I tickled him.

How much he depended on me. How often he seemed awed by my maternal wisdom. *Now, I reasoned, he's grown and doesn't need me any longer.* But later that week, I got a pleasant surprise. The phone rang. It was Joe. "Mom," he said, "I just wanted to say thanks for all you do, and . . . I miss you. Is it okay if I come home next weekend and bring my dirty laundry?" My heart smiled. "Sure, Joe, and I love you too." Thank You, Lord, for small connections.

> *For everything there is a season, and a time to every matter under heaven.*
> —ECCLESIASTES 3:1 RSV

Dear God . . .

It has taken me a long time to understand the power of my words. I once thought it was my duty to let people know when they were wrong. After all, somebody had to do it. I would interrupt right in the middle of what they were saying to correct them. When they were proud of an accomplishment, I was quick to point out how it could have been done better. And when they had exciting news about a venture they were launching, I would bring up all the reasons why it might fail. They don't call it playing the devil's advocate for nothing. Then I met Agnes. She was even better at discouragement than I. She cut me down whenever I opened my mouth. Sometimes You get our attention by showing us our faults through another's similarities. It was a rude awakening. I didn't like the resemblance, but it

forced me to see that playing devil's advocate is
not in Your likeness. So with Your help, I began
to change. Now I speak words of truth—Your
Truth. I tell others that if they have faith,
anything is possible, for You provide us with
everything we need to make our dreams come
true. Now I affirm instead of discourage. I no
longer tell people what they can't accomplish. I
tell them that life is filled with possibilities . . .
that we have a loving Father whose great
pleasure it is to give us His kingdom.

-187-

*May the words of my mouth and
the meditation of my heart be
pleasing in your sight, O LORD,
my Rock and my Redeemer.*
—PSALM 19:14

the answer

Dear God . . .

My grandson Shaun asked why so many
people hurt each other. I was stunned to realize
I had no answer, but I knew, with his inquiring
mind, he would press for an explanation. I
thought about it, realizing that as a child his
age, I had lived a rather sheltered life. My world
was gentler. Shaun's world is very different. I,
too, question why people are so aggressive, so
hurtful. Finally I said, "I know it can be
frightening." "But, Grammie," he persisted,
"how can we be sure it won't happen to us?" I
said to him, "Shaun, why don't we pray about
it." He folded his small hands and bowed his
head. We prayed, "Dear Lord, we come to You
for answers to our world's problems. Why do
people hurt each other instead of helping one
another to live a better life? How can we be
safe in such a world?" We were silent and then

Shaun said, "Maybe that's why God gave us faith. You know, Grammie, no matter what happens, we can always run to God, and He'll swoop us up in His arms. We'll be safe there." I smiled at my grandson's wisdom and realized he was right. The faith You give us will overcome any adversity. "That's right, Shaun, when danger is near, all we need do is run to God and He'll swoop us up in His everlasting arms."

–189–

Little children were brought to Jesus for him to place his hands on them and pray for them.

—MATTHEW 19:13

the tree heart

Dear God . . .

I walked along the wooded path as spring danced among the budding trees and bent low to breathe life into the flowering earth. The forest echoed with sounds of newly created life, and I knew I was witnessing the sacred ritual of earth renewing itself. I was suddenly aware that time, as we use it, is a futile attempt to rule the world. We mortals plan our days as if we own them—as if total control affords us veneration. I lingered as I came before the mammoth oak tree with its outstretched arms. Surely this ancient living monument had witnessed the passage of many years. As I drew closer to the tree, I noticed a heart carved into its trunk with the testimonial "BL loves CW." Time has not erased this decree of devotion. I wondered about these two lovers who displayed their feelings for each other, so the world would not forget them.

What part of time had they shared? Did they marry? Did they raise a family? Did they go on to find other loves? The tree carving is a living symbol of the meaning of life, isn't it, Father? Someday, time will give way to the rhythm of eternity. And all that will be left is Truth—the truth that love endures beyond this life, that sharing our love is primary, and that the love we share is carved into the tree of life as an eternal image of who we are.

Forgive, and deal with each man according to all he does, since you know his heart (for you alone know the hearts of men).

—2 CHRONICLES 6:30

Dear God . . .

Some of the deepest mysteries in life are our nightly dreams. As I recall my dreams, I am amazed at how real they seem. When I drift off to sleep and enter my dream world, it feels as if I've walked right through a painting on the wall and into another world. That painting is sometimes dark and foreboding, but it often contains splashes of brightness and truth. I meet people I've not seen in years. I fly in midair without benefit of wings. I solve problems. I sometimes meet loved ones who have passed on, feeling the love we shared in life. When I awaken, I find myself wondering which world is reality. Dreams are such adventures. I don't know the reasons that You've created our subconscious to fashion these animated stories, but I do know they have a purpose in working out life's frustrations and fears and in giving us

some answers we've struggled to find. I live in
two worlds—the world of sleep and the waking
world. It's fascinating to experience my dreams
and to walk back through that painting in the
morning to a brand new world of living.
Perhaps dreams are a way of sweeping the mind
of debris while we sleep, so our thoughts and
feelings can reflect You more authentically.
Whatever the reasons, I thank You, Father, that
You take care of so many things in life, even
without my awareness. I don't need to know all
the answers. I've only to trust You.

–193–

Send forth your light and your truth,
let them guide me.
—PSALM 43:3

Dear God . . .

Today I am so proud of my daughter walking across the stage to receive her high school diploma. There were times when I thought this moment would never come. She had such a struggle all through school. In the earlier grades, I worked with her every evening, so her reading skills would improve. We both would be exhausted and frustrated at the end of those sessions. I accused her of not trying. She would cry and tell me I was too hard on her. Then we discovered she was severely dyslexic and that was the reason she had trouble keeping up with her reading. I felt awful that I had pushed her so hard when it never could have helped. We both felt relief when her challenge was named, and we knew our struggles had not been because she wasn't trying. Then came the wonderful discovery of her fine creative ability.

She can draw and paint and sculpt better than most. She has talents that You placed inside her the day she was created, and she excels in those gifts. As her self-esteem grew, her work at school became more tolerable. She still struggles with reading, but now she knows that she has great talents, gifts that others sometimes envy. Through all of this, I have learned to appreciate others for who they are and for the unique gifts each has to offer, for within each of us are special gifts just waiting to be unwrapped.

Do not neglect your gift. . . . Be diligent in these matters; give yourself wholly to them, so that everyone may see your progress.
1 TIMOTHY 4:14-15

Dear God . . .

You must shake Your head at times as You watch the antics of Your blundering children. We get all puffed up with our own importance and revel in our strength of mind and body. Our heads swell as we bask in our accomplishments. How bright and creative we are, or so we think, until we fall flat on our faces like dolls at play. Who do we really think pulls the strings of life? How can we get so inflated over our achievements without giving You the credit? Surely, without Your master hand working the strings, we would perform our puppet dance to a sad song. Looking back, the history of life records the story of how the stage was set and the melodrama has played out. The older I become, the more I laugh at our antics—Your blundering children. No matter how long we live or how educated we become, the uniqueness we desire comes from giving You the credit for our successful performance. Our dancing feet must keep time with the music of Your love. I feel like opening my arms full length and shouting to Heaven, "Here I am, Lord, Your foolish child. I come to You with trust in my heart. Pick up the strands of my life, and choreograph my steps, so my puppet dance will be worthy to dance in step with You."

–197–

It is God who makes both us and you stand firm in Christ. He anointed us, set his seal of ownership on us, and put his Spirit in our hearts as a deposit, guaranteeing what is to come.

—2 CORINTHIANS 1:21-22

the threshold

Dear God . . .

I prayed about doing volunteer work, and
You led me to the hospital—not only for what I
could do for others, but for what they could do
for me. I didn't know that it would change my
attitude about life. I was only qualified for
office work, but thankfully You led me to the
rehabilitation ward. There, I met people, young
and old, who were learning to reach beyond
their limits. It was a painful process for them,
and I became personally involved in the
progress of each person. I was especially
amazed at the children. At first, I felt sorry for
them, their young lives challenged in ways that
made me want to cry. But as I saw these
courageous spirits stretch their limbs and reach
for a higher potential, my own spirit began to
grow. They taught me not to settle for perceived
limitations, for beyond the threshold of pain

and endurance is another world—a world that
You understand, Father. There is no need for me
to understand it. I've only to let go of doubt
and fear, and You will take me to that place
where limits vanish like the morning dew with
the passionate kiss of the sun. So, though I may
be middle-aged, there is nothing that can keep
me from my full potential—if I don't let it. I'll
not look back at past failures, nor nurture the
seeds of other's negative opinions. I look
forward to all that You have planned for me—
in this world of miraculous possibilities.

-199-

Forget the former things,
do not dwell on the past.
—ISAIAH 43:18

an attitude of living

Dear God . . .

When I was young and rebellious, I would watch Mom as she prayed and wonder what she said to You, Lord. When I grew older, it was all she could do to keep me in church. I went mostly so Dad wouldn't get upset. Before she went to bed at night, Mom would always ask if I had said my prayers. One day I asked just how many times a day I was supposed to pray. She told me, "You don't cut your prayers into sections and say you've done your quota. Prayer is an attitude of living." I didn't know what she meant then. Now, looking back, I understand what Mom was saying. We come to You when we awaken in the mornings, again at mealtime, and before closing our eyes at night. But a lot of living happens between dawn and dusk, and all that we do during our day should be part of our prayer life—an attitude of love. If we lived as if each day might be our last, our lives would be more of a living prayer. Leaving this world is not just a possibility, it's a given. I vow to pray in everything I do and say. Then, at the end of this life, when we meet in Heaven, Lord, You'll know me by my attitude, and You'll whisper, "Amen, my good servant."

–201–

Jesus told his disciples a parable to show them that they should always pray and not give up.

—LUKE 18:1

topical index

about the author

Peggy Rooney is the Secretary to Cardinal Hickey, Archbishop Emeritus of Washington, D.C. She has worked for the Archdiocese since 1989, first in the Communications Office, then  as Secretary to the Monsignor. Her professional experience over the past thirty years has spanned a variety of jobs, from bagging groceries at the supermarket to computer administration.

As a single mom with limited resources, she often saw God provide awe-inspiring miracles in her everyday life. Peggy enjoys writing, as she draws on her personal experiences, struggles, and successes for inspiration. She also likes to sing and play the guitar, composing inspirational music and lyrics to perform during liturgical celebrations.

Peggy is the proud mother of four grown children and grandmother of eight grandchildren. She resides in Greenbelt, Maryland.